DK EYEWITNESS

T0067039

TOP 10
DUBROVNIK
AND THE DALMATIAN COAST

Top 10 Dubrovnik and the Dalmatian Coast Highlights

The Top 10 of Everything

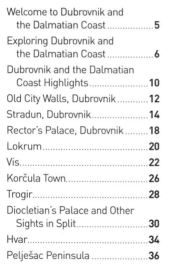

CONTENTS

Dubrovnik and the Dalmatian Coast Area by Area

Streetsmart

Within each Top 10 list in this book, no hierarchy of quality or popularity is implied. All 10 are, in the editor's opinion, of roughly equal merit.

Title page, front cover and spine *Picturesque Stari Grad with its terracotta rooftops*
Back cover, clockwise from top left *Vis Island; Interior of St. Domnius Cathedral; Sunset over Dubrovnik; Stari Grad; Street in Old Town*

The rate at which the world is changing is constantly keeping the DK Eyewitness team on our toes. While we've worked hard to ensure that this edition of Dubrovnik and the Dalmatian Coast is accurate and up-to-date, we know that opening hours alter, standards shift, prices fluctuate, places close and new ones pop up in their stead. So, if you notice we've got something wrong or left something out, we want to hear about it. Please get in touch at **travelguides@dk.com**

Welcome to
Dubrovnik and the Dalmatian Coast

An ancient walled town jutting seaward from a mountainous coast, Dubrovnik is one of the Mediterranean's most beguiling destinations. It stands on a dramatic stretch of coastline, with historic ports wedged into its bays and inlets, and a clutch of idyllic islands just a short ferry ride offshore. With DK Eyewitness Top 10 Dubrovnik and the Dalmatian Coast, it's yours to explore.

Enclosed by the **Old City Walls**, Dubrovnik is packed with fine sights such as the ornate **Rector's Palace**, the impressive **Franciscan Monastery** and **Stradun**, the road that has long been the city's beating heart. Renaissance town houses and some of Croatia's most cosmopolitan bars and restaurants are squeezed into the narrow alleys that spiral away from Stradun – making Dubrovnik a medieval city with a decidedly contemporary edge.

Northwest of Dubrovnik, the bustling port of **Split** started out as the retirement home of Roman emperor Diocletian, whose palace still forms the city's vibrant core. Ferries run from Split to the Dalmatian islands of **Hvar**, **Korčula** and **Vis**, which have chic nightspots, lush olive groves and a variety of beaches. Wherever you go, you will find crystal clear seas – perfect for swimming, snorkelling or kayaking.

Whether you're visiting for a weekend, a week, or longer, our Top 10 guide brings together the best of everything the region has to offer, from Dubrovnik's city walls to the most secluded island beaches. The guide has useful tips throughout, from seeking out what's free to splashing out on the best Dalmatian wines, plus six easy-to-follow itineraries designed to tie together a clutch of sights in a short space of time. Add inspiring photography and detailed maps, and you've got the essential pocket-sized travel companion. **Enjoy the book, and enjoy Dubrovnik and the Dalmatian Coast**.

Clockwise from top: Bay near Hvar town, lion sculpture in a portal at Trogir's Cathedral of St Lawrence, the Old Harbour in Dubrovnik, Orebić town, Dubrovnik lace, Neretva Delta, a pavement café in Dubrovnik

Exploring Dubrovnik and the Dalmatian Coast

The area surrounding Dubrovnik features historic cities, wild landscapes and crystal-clear seas. To make the most of your stay and help you to get a flavour of this fascinating region, here are some ideas for two-day and seven-day Dalmatian jaunts.

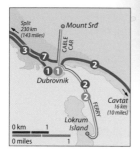

Dubrovnik's 14th-century **Franciscan Monastery** dominates the western end of the city.

Two Days in Dubrovnik

Day ❶

MORNING

Begin with a circuit of **Dubrovnik's city walls** (see pp12–13) to take in some fabulous views of the Old City. Continue with a stroll down the **Stradun** (see pp14–15), Dubrovnik's set-piece main street.

AFTERNOON

Relive the glory of the Dubrovnik Republic with a visit to the **Rector's Palace** (see pp18–19). Next, soak up the historic atmosphere of Dubrovnik by wandering through the **Pustijerna quarter** (see p70).

Day ❷

MORNING

Admire Renaissance artworks at the **Franciscan Monastery** (see pp16–17)

before taking the cable car to **Mount Srđ** (see p71) to see the stunning panorama of the coast.

AFTERNOON

Take a boat to the island of **Lokrum** (see pp20–21), a self-contained world of semi-wild gardens and stunning coastal paths. On your return, admire the sculptures in the **Museum of Modern Art** (see p67).

Seven Days in Dalmatia

Day ❶

Follow day 1 of the two-day Dubrovnik itinerary.

Day ❷

Spend the morning exploring **Lokrum** (see pp20–21), a beautiful island of lush greenery and rocky bays. Afterwards, head south to

Set around the Cathedral of St Stephen, the main square in Hvar town is lined with impressive Renaissance buildings.

Key
- Two-day itinerary
- Seven-day itinerary

Cavtat *(see p96)* for a late lunch on the palm-shaded waterfront. Return to Dubrovnik via **Sokol grad** *(see p97)* for a taste of stark inland scenery.

Day ❸

Travel from Dubrovnik to Split, pausing to enjoy the long pebble beaches of the **Makarska Riviera** *(see pp86–93)*. Spend a couple of hours exploring the medieval town of **Trogir** *(see pp28–9)* before ending the day in Split. Spend the evening strolling the bustling **Diocletian's Palace** quarter *(see pp30–31)*.

Day ❹

Leave Split by ferry for the laid-back island of **Vis** *(see pp22–3)*. Stroll around Vis town before crossing the island to the historic fishing port of Komiža. In the afternoon, take a fast boat from Komiža harbour to the

islet of **Biševo** *(see p81)* and its Blue Cave. Return to Komiža for a sumptuous seafood dinner.

Day ❺

At certain times, you can travel directly by catamaran from Vis town to **Hvar town** *(see p34)*. Otherwise, return to Split and take the car ferry to Hvar island's main port, Stari Grad. Hire a vehicle to tour the island *(see pp34–5)*, taking in the pretty port of **Jelsa**, as well as the Renaissance splendours of Hvar town. The town's chic bars and trendy clubs may well keep you occupied until morning.

Day ❻

Providing you book in advance, the morning catamaran from Hvar town will get you to **Korčula town** *(see pp26–7)* early enough to take a pre-lunch amble through this historic peninsula settlement. Grab a bite at **Adio Mare** *(see p83)* before heading to the sandy beaches of **Lumbarda** *(see p49)*, just outside Korčula town, for a spot of swimming and sunbathing.

Day ❼

Take the ferry from Korčula to Orebić and drive along the **Pelješac Peninsula** *(see pp36–7)*, stopping for lunch at the gourmet town of Ston. Afterwards, continue to Dubrovnik, arriving in time for an evening cable-car trip up **Mount Srd** *(see p71)*.

Some of the region's best beaches are in Orebić, on the Pelješac Peninsula.

Top 10 Dubrovnik and the Dalmatian Coast Highlights

Aerial view of Dubrovnik's historic town and the island of Lokrum

TOP 10 Dubrovnik and the Dalmatian Coast Highlights

The Dalmatian coast is one of Europe's most stunning escapes. Long stretches of glorious shoreline are framed between limestone mountains and the Adriatic, where hundreds of islands await exploration. The coastline is punctuated by a series of lively towns and cities, in which the region's long and eclectic history comes alive in wonderfully preserved "old cores".

1 Old City Walls, Dubrovnik

For centuries, these remarkable city walls have afforded Dubrovnik protection. Today they allow visitors a bird's-eye view of this impressive city (see pp12–13).

2 Stradun, Dubrovnik

Along its polished expanse, Dubrovnik's pedestrianized main thoroughfare has churches, palaces, shops, fountains and pavement cafés (see pp14–17).

3 Rector's Palace, Dubrovnik

Under the Republic of Ragusa, the city's figurehead presided here, amid Gothic and Renaissance architecture. This impressive palace has been reinvented as a museum and cultural venue (see pp18–19).

4 Lokrum

Mediterranean gardens combine with rocky beaches and untrammelled nature to make this small island an essential trip from Dubrovnik, just to the north (see pp20–21).

5 Vis

This compact island is bursting with history and natural beauty, with the central massif of Mount Hum book-ended by the charming ports of Komiža and Vis town. Add the widest range of seafood in the Adriatic, and Vis is also a foodie haven *(see pp22–3)*.

Korčula Town **6**

It is not, as some claim, the birthplace of Marco Polo, but that doesn't make Korčula town any less sublime. Set on its own peninsula, Korčula is a perfect example of a fortified medieval town *(see pp26–7)*.

7 Trogir

Situated on its own island, this perfectly preserved old city dazzles with churches, palaces and one of Europe's most striking cathedrals, whose beauty is recognized by UNESCO *(see pp28–9)*.

Diocletian's Palace, Split **8**

The palatial, UNESCO World Heritage-listed retirement home of Emperor Diocletian forms the frenetic heart of the dashing Mediterranean city of Split *(see pp30–33)*.

BOSNIA & ERZEGOVINA

Metković

Opuzen

Ston • Mali Ston

Mljet

1 **2** **3**
Dubrovnik

4 Cavtat

Lokrum

km 25

miles 25

Herceg-Novi

9 Hvar

Of all Croatia's islands, Hvar arguably offers most variety. Swanky marinas and fashionable bars and restaurants sit alongside family resorts, ancient villages and secluded beaches *(see pp34–5)*.

10 Pelješac Peninsula

A mountainous finger of land poking west from the Dalmatian coast, Pelješac is ideal for beachcombers and offers great wine and seafood *(see pp36–7)*.

🔟⭐ Old City Walls, Dubrovnik

Measuring up to 6 m (20 ft) thick and 22 m (72 ft) high, Dubrovnik's city walls are a stunning sight. A cradle of stone, they helped protect one of Europe's most perfectly preserved medieval cities, as well as safeguarding the independence of the city-state for centuries. Running from the steep cliffs in the north to the Adriatic in the south, they proved impenetrable to pirates and potential conquerors until 1806 when the French occupied the republic of Dubrovnik. Two years later, in 1808, the Republic was abolished.

3 Ploče Gate
The bridge leading to the Ploče Gate, on the eastern walls, offers new arrivals tantalizing glimpses of the city and the old port.

4 Revelin Fort
Near the eastern walls, this 16th-century fortress is used for exhibitions, plus music and dancing in summer.

1 Pile Gate
This entrance **(above)** to the Old City leads, via a drawbridge, down on to the Stradun. Look out for the figure of Dubrovnik's patron saint, St Blaise, above the gate and, a little further on, a more modern depiction of him by Ivan Meštrović.

2 Minčeta Fort
North of the Pile Gate, steep steps lead up to an impressive fort **(below)**. The sunset views from this 15th-century bastion justify the exertion to reach it.

5 Bokar Fort
This Renaissance fort designed by Michelozzo Michelozzi, watches over the city's original port. From here, the Lovrijenac Fortress **(above)** is also visible.

6 St Luke's Fortress
Overlooking the port, this 13th-century fortification is a semicircular bastion where sea-facing cannons were housed. Part of the fortress is now occupied by a restaurant and bar.

Aerial view of Old City

LIBERTAS
Dubrovnik's daunting city walls are just part of the reason why the Republic of Ragusa enjoyed centuries of independence, at a time when the Venetians and Ottomans were vying for territory all around the Adriatic. Machiavelli would have applauded the skill of the republic's negotiators as they played off the various powers against each other, dipping into the city's bountiful gold reserves when all else failed. The word proudly flown on their flag was *Libertas* (freedom).

Map of the Old City Walls

10 Rooftops

The legacy of the 1991–2 siege (see p41) is evident from the stretch of wall around the old port. From here the contrast between the charming, original roof tiles and the newer replacements, imported from France and Slovenia, is very easy to see.

7 Maritime Museum

Part of St John's Fortress is a museum (see pp46–7) that sheds light on the Republic of Ragusa's rich and eclectic maritime heritage. The exhibits include a large collection of model ships, sepia photographs of the port and historic maps.

8 Boat Trip

For a completely different perspective of Dubrovnik's walls, join a tour boat or hire a local water taxi (both leave from the old port) and skirt around the base of the city (below), where the Adriatic swishes against the rocks and the ramparts soar menacingly upward.

9 St John's Fort

This fortification protected the old port from advancing enemy ships and was, in its time, at the cutting edge of military technology. Begun in 1346, it was added to well into the 16th century.

NEED TO KNOW

MAP E9 ■ Access the walls from the Stradun (next to the Pile Gate), by St John's Fort and St Luke's Fortress

Open Apr & early Sep: 8am–6:30pm daily (May & Aug: to 7pm; Jun & Jul: to 7:30pm; mid–late Sep: to 6pm; early Oct: to 5:30pm; mid–late Oct: to 5pm); Nov–Mar: 9am–3pm daily

Adm €35 (Mar–Oct), €15 (Nov–Feb); children €15 (Mar–Oct), €5 (Nov–Feb); audio guide available

Maritime Museum: MAP H10; 020 323 904; open Apr–Oct: 9am–6pm Thu–Tue; Nov–Mar: 9am–4pm Thu–Tue; adm €10 (incl entry to other sites); children/students €7; family €25

■ Buža (see p74), outside the southern walls, has great views. From the Jesuit Church, follow the "cold drinks" sign.

■ The walls are crowded in summer, so arrive early to avoid queues.

🔟 ⭐ Stradun, Dubrovnik

The sweeping Stradun, also known as the Placa, is Dubrovnik's main thoroughfare, cutting a pedestrianized swathe through the Old City. It was formed when the narrow channel that separated the Slavic settlement of Dubrovnik on the mainland from the Roman settlement on the island of Raus was filled in during the 12th century. Today this limestone walkway, with its shops, cafés and restaurants, buzzes with visitors.

THE EARTHQUAKE OF 1667

This earthquake tore the heart out of Gothic and Renaissance Dubrovnik, killing 2,500 citizens and destroying many key buildings. This terrible tragedy led to the construction of one of the most impressive Baroque cities in Europe. Carefully planned to sit within the protective confines of the sturdy city walls, it resisted all intruders until the arrival of Napoleonic troops in the early 19th century.

1 Sponza Palace
The inscription, "We are forbidden to cheat and use false measures, and when I weigh goods, God weighs me," reveals this early 16th-century palace's former role as customs house and mint **(above)**. Today it is home to the State Archives.

2 Café Culture
Join the locals for a drink and watch the world go by. Many cafés set tables out at the first glimpse of sunshine, but getting a seat can be an ordeal at the height of summer.

4 Shutters and Lamps
For a controlled piece of town planning, look at the window shutters and the lamps along the Stradun. They are all the same shade of green, giving a cohesion rare in European cities today.

The bustling Stradun

3 Onofrio's Large Fountain
Damaged in the siege of 1991–2, this 15th-century fountain **(below)** has been restored. It is named after the architect of the city's water-supply system.

5 Orlando's Column
Mystery surrounds the statue that guards the spot where the Stradun unfurls into Luža Square. Some locals claim that Orlando was a legendary knight who saved the city from disaster when he fought off menacing pirates in the 8th century.

6 Onofrio's Little Fountain

Tucked into a building by the Rector's Palace, this "little sister" to Onofrio's Large Fountain often goes unnoticed. It dates from the 15th century.

Map of the Stradun

9 Clocktower

This striking timepiece (left) dates from the 15th century. Overhauled in 1929, the duo of bell strikers visible today are copies. The originals are housed in the city's Sponza Palace.

7 Church of St Saviour

The staid Renaissance façade does little to hint at the colour inside. Here regular concerts and art exhibitions are held, often with work by modern Dalmatian artists.

8 Franciscan Monastery

The dark cloisters and lush vegetation of this 14th-century monastery (see p16) conjure up echoes of the Dubrovnik of old, as do the fascinating exhibits of the Monastery Museum (see p17). Make sure you arrive early to avoid the crowds.

10 Church of St Blaise

This church (below) sits at the top of the Stradun. Inside, Dubrovnik's patron saint, St Blaise, cradles a model of the city showing what it looked like before the earthquake of 1667.

Franciscan Monastery, Stradun

The inner courtyard of the monastery

1 Inner Courtyard
Step into this inner sanctum to view the cloisters and admire the spectacular balustrade that frames the courtyard.

2 Romanesque Cloisters
Mihoje Brajkov's magnificent 14th-century cloisters, with their graceful double-pillared columns, deserve a close look. These can be visited between 9am and 6pm.

3 Frescoes
The life of St Francis and his animals is depicted in the frescoes that line the cloisters.

4 Bell Tower
The dome-topped bell tower dominating the western end of the Stradun dates from the 14th century and features Gothic and Romanesque elements. Its majestic presence towers over the monastery courtyard.

5 Pharmacy
The monastery is home to one of the oldest pharmacies in Europe, with treatments and products dating from the 15th century. The dispensary is still operational everyday except Sunday.

6 Church of St Francis
Most of the original 14th-century church was destroyed by the 1667 earthquake. Remarkable features in this 17th-century reconstruction include the lavish marble altars and the ornate organ framed by cherubs.

7 Library
The monastery is home to Croatia's largest collection of historical manuscripts, with over 3,000, dating from the early Middle Ages.

8 Portraits
The library walls are adorned with portraits of some of the city's most celebrated citizens, including Marin Getaldić, a 17th-century mathematician and physicist.

9 Ivan Gundulić Memorial
A plaque on the north wall of the church commemorates the poet Ivan Gundulić (1589–1638), who is buried in the church.

10 Gothic Portal
A *Pietà* by brothers Petar and Leonardo Petrović crowns the southern portal, which is all that remains of the original 14th-century church.

Pietà by the Petrović brothers

Franciscan Monastery Museum

1 Dubrovnik Painting
The background of Nikola Božidarević's *Madonna and Child* painting shows how medieval Dubrovnik looked before the devastating earthquake of 1667.

2 Missile Damage
On 6 December 1991, known locally as "Black Tuesday", Serbian missiles rained down on Dubrovnik. Two shell-holes have been left in the museum walls to serve as reminders of the damage sustained by the monastery.

Stone relief of St Francis

3 War Record
Inconspicuously located below the painting of Dubrovnik is a book cataloguing the devastation caused by the 54 direct hits upon the monastery during the siege of the city in 1991–2.

4 Missiles
Tucked into a corner, by a bench near the entrance to the museum, lie the casings of some of the missiles that wrought destruction on this tranquil space.

5 St Blaise's Foot
The most prized possession in the reliquary collection is this foot of St Blaise, preserved in a boot-like gold-and-silver case.

6 Osman
One of the treasures of the monastery's library is an 18th-century transcript of Ivan Gundulić's *Osman*. Heralded as the poet's masterpiece, it celebrates a famous Slavic victory over the Turks.

7 Potions and Poisons
Set in a recreation of the monastery's original pharmacy are row upon row of measuring instruments, traditional remedies and some lethal poisons.

8 St Francis
The medieval stone relief of St Francis, above the museum entrance, appears to be casting a protective eye over his domain.

9 Stone Reliefs
A small open space to one side of the museum contains odd remnants of carved masonry from the building, including gargoyles and segments of old gravestones.

10 Religious Exhibits
The museum houses several 15th- and 16th-century icons, a crucifix by Blaž Jurjev Trogiranin dating from 1428, as well as a beautiful 15th-century polyptych by Lovro Marinov Dobričević, which features a portrait of St Blaise.

A 16th-century icon depicting the Annunciation

⭐ Rector's Palace, Dubrovnik

Rectors, the nominal head of the Republic of Ragusa's government, were elected by the city's Major Council and served for one month at a time, becoming eligible for reelection after two years. While in office, they could only leave their palace on official business. The current Gothic-Renaissance building dates from 1435, when the original medieval castellum was damaged in a gunpowder explosion. Today, the Rector's Palace houses the Cultural History Museum.

Gothic Portico ③

The ornately carved portico **(right)** was built using stone from the Dalmatian island of Korčula. In the middle of the parade of Gothic columns and capitals are three in the Renaissance style.

① Stairs

The main Baroque staircase **(above)** leading up to the first floor is adorned with three lifelike hands on each rail. They were used only on ceremonial occasions, when the Rector received visitors.

④ Gundulić Portrait

This is one of the few portraits in existence of Dubrovnik's most celebrated poet, Ivan Gundulić (1589–1638).

Statue of Miho Pracat ②

Taking pride of place in the atrium is Pietro Giacometti's 17th-century statue of shipping magnate Miho Pracat **(right)**, from the nearby island of Lopud. Dying without an heir, Pracat left his wealth to the Republic of Ragusa.

⑤ Atrium

A compact open-air space **(left)** that offers a suitably grand welcome to visitors, the historical atrium also serves as a unique venue for many cultural events, such as recitals by the Dubrovnik Symphony Orchestra.

AN EXPLOSIVE HISTORY

In addition to being the abode of the head of the Republic of Ragusa, as well as the site of the law courts and prison, the Rector's Palace also contained a gunpowder store. This decision on the part of the authorities unfortunately resulted in several explosions that caused damage to the building. It was only after a second disastrous explosion in 1463 that the city's leaders finally made the decision to move the gunpowder elsewhere.

6 Statues of St Blaise

The sculptures of St Blaise in the museum here afford visitors a rare opportunity to get up close to the city's patron saint. Most other sculptural depictions are well above head height, or behind distant glass in his eponymous church *(see p45)*.

Key
First floor
Ground floor

Plan of the Rector's Palace

7 Prison Cells

The ground floor was once the Republic of Ragusa's courtroom and prison. The dank, gloomy cells hint at the harsh treatment of inmates, who mostly relied on friends and family for food and water.

8 Inscription

The notice in Latin at the top of the stairs would have served as a reminder for the Grand Council members of their duty to focus, not on personal concerns, but only on public and civic matters.

NEED TO KNOW

MAP G9 ■ Pred Dvorom 3
■ 020 321 422

Open Apr–Oct: 9am–6pm daily (Nov–Mar: to 4pm Thu–Tue); closed 1 Jan, 3 Feb, 25 Dec

Adm €15; children/students €8; family €35

■ The Gradska Kavana *(see p74)* is a café fit for a rector, with stunning views across the Luža Square and down the Stradun on one side and out on to the historic old port on the other.

■ The windows on the first floor make a perfect spot for photographing both the cathedral and the displays of folk dancing that sometimes take place in the street below.

9 Sedan Chairs

A collection of 18th-century sedan chairs **(right)**, is found on the first floor and at other locations in the palace. These chairs offer a hint of the opulence of the city's nobility.

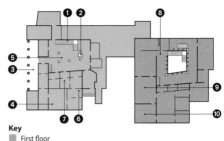

10 Rector's Study

In the study, one of the most elegant and graceful rooms in the palace, visitors are able to admire the 16th-century painting *The Baptism of Christ* by Mihajlo Hamzić (1460–1518) and a cabinet painted by Luca Giordano (1634–1705).

🔟⭐ Lokrum

A short distance offshore, the lush green island of Lokrum is a real contrast to the bustle of Dubrovnik. A protected natural site, the island is covered with a special reserve of forest vegetation, while its coast offers some of Dubrovnik's best sunbathing and swimming. The former Benedictine monastery, which was turned into a holiday home by Austrian Archduke Maximilian and later used as a set for the TV show *Game of Thrones*, provides a strong historical focus.

① The Boat Landing

Exploration of the island begins at the boat landing **(right)**, over-looked by the Forest Ranger's House. A peach-coloured villa built in Archduke Maximilian's time, the lodge is now a park information centre and exhibition space.

② The "Dead Sea" Lake

One of Lokrum's most popular bathing areas is this unusually buoyant saltwater lake **(below)** just inland from the island's southeastern tip.

③ Benedictine Monastery

Founded in the 11th century, Lokrum's Benedictine Monastery was a major seat of learning until its dissolution in 1798. Archduke Maximilian bought it in 1859 but preserved many of its features – notably the elegant cloisters, where you will now find a restaurant and café.

④ Game of Thrones Exhibition

A wing of the monastery is largely devoted to the TV show *Game of Thrones*, scenes of which were shot in the cloisters. There is an interactive map of locations seen in the series and a selection of stage props, including the iron throne used by the rulers of King's Landing.

NEED TO KNOW

MAP H6

■ www.lokrum.hr

Passenger boats run from the harbour in Dubrovnik's Old City every hour (every half-hour in peak season) from May to November, taking less than 15 minutes.

Return ticket for the boat €7; adm €27, children €5; all of the island's attractions remain open from the arrival of the first boat (10am, depending on season) to the departure of the last (6pm).

···············

■ Just up from the boat landing and enclosed by well-trimmed hedges is a pleasant open-air café, frequented by the island's free-roaming peacocks.

■ It is forbidden to pick plants or to stay on the island overnight.

■ There is a restaurant in the former monastery building, but Lokrum is a great place for a picnic too. Choose a bench beside the Path of Paradise, or spread your blanket on the olive-shaded lawns beside the monastery.

7 The Gardens of Maximilian

South of the monastery buildings are beautiful terraces featuring geometrically laid-out box hedges **(left)**. They were planted by Archduke Maximilian, who planned to turn the whole island into a park.

GAME OF THRONES

The famous fantasy TV series *Game of Thrones* was filmed in Dubrovnik between 2011 and 2018, from the second to the final season of the show. The city itself doubled as the fictional capital city King's Landing, with many of Dubrovnik's trademark features (such as the medieval walls and Lovrijenac Fortress) becoming an integral part of the show's visual style. Other locations included Lokrum's monastery cloisters, which were used for a garden-party scene in Qarth, and Klis Fortress near Split (*see p88*), which was the ideal setting for the hilltop city of Meereen.

5 Botanical Gardens

A striking collection of plants from Australia, Africa and South America fill this large enclosure, established in 1959 by the National Academy of Science and Art. The garden, part of the Institute for Marine and Coastal Research, features over 70 kinds of eucalyptus and towering cacti.

8 Path of Paradise

Made up of three avenues, the Path of Paradise stretches from the lower part of the island towards Fort Royal. It was planted during the time of Archduke Maximilian, when it would have been bordered on both sides by a row of Mediterranean cypresses and stone curbs.

Map of Lokrum Island

6 Fort Royal

Located on the summit of 96-m (315-ft) Glavica Hill, Lokrum's highest point, this circular fortress **(below)** was built by the French in 1806, straight after their takeover of the Adriatic coast. It offers fantastic views overlooking a forest of Aleppo pine trees, the sea and Dubrovnik beyond.

9 Naturist Beach

The terraced rock formations east of the The Gardens of Maximilian have plenty of stony platforms ideal for sunbathing. A cult spot among nudists for decades, the eastern shore is now a designated naturist bathing area.

10 Ruined Basilica

Within the Benedictine monastery complex are the impressive remains of a three-aisled Romanesque basilica. Dating from the 12th century, it attests to the importance of Lokrum in the religious life of the Republic of Ragusa.

TOP 10 ⭐ Vis

Compact, mountainous and full of history, Vis is one of the Adriatic's most compelling island destinations. Further from the mainland than Croatia's other major islands, it has long held strategic importance for those wishing to control the Adriatic, including the British and Austro-Hungarian Empires. Vis opened up to tourism in the early 1990s while it was still serving as a major Yugoslav army base, but it retains an unspoiled, non-commercialized feel.

Vis Town ①
Stretching along the shores of a broad bay, the island's main settlement features a wealth of ancient Greek, Roman and Renaissance remains. The seafront is packed with yachts in the summer **(right)**, and there are some wonderful restaurants serving local specialities.

② Mount Hum
At 587 m (1,926 ft) above sea level, Vis's highest point offers stunning Adriatic views, with the port of Komiža below and the islands of Biševo, Jabuka and Svetac to the west. On a clear day, you can see all the way to Italy's coast.

③ Komiža
Curled round a steep-sided bay **(above)**, the former capital of the Adriatic anchovy-fishing industry is today a charming port.

④ King George III Fortress
Built by the British in 1813, and currently serving as a bar, restaurant and nightclub, this sturdy hilltop fortress contains a small museum devoted to the island's military history and offers sweeping views from its tower.

⑤ Kut
Squeezed into a corner of the bay, this quiet suburb of Vis town was where the 16th-century nobles of Hvar built their summer houses. Still filled with elegant stone villas overlooking narrow streets, it preserves an aristocratic air.

⑥ Submarine Pens
Built to house the Yugoslav navy's pocket submarines, these concrete tunnels **(below)** outside Vis town are popular with nautical tourists, who can sail small craft inside. They are also accessible on foot or by bike.

7 Tito's Cave

Vis served as the headquarters of Yugoslavia's Partisan movement in 1944, when Marshal Tito presided over top-level meetings in this cave on the side of Mount Hum. It is now bare, with the exception of a few inscriptions, but it is still a popular site of political pilgrimage.

Map of Vis

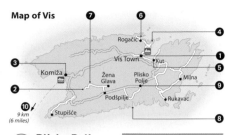

9 Plisko Polje

This village sits on the edge of a lush green plain that produces most of the island's fruit, vegetables and wine – particularly Vugava, the dry white wine that is indigenous to Vis.

10 The Blue Cave

Excursion boats and motor dinghies speed across the water from Komiža to the island of Biševo, where the unique Blue Cave is one of Croatia's most visited natural wonders, illuminated by refracted turquoise light.

WARTIME VIS

During World War II, Dalmatia was occupied by Italian forces. The Adriatic coast was liberated by Yugoslav Partisans, led by Josip Broz Tito, and reunited with the rest of Croatia. From June to September 1944, the headquarters of Tito's Partisan movement was on Vis, which became heavily garrisoned and protected by Britain and the US. The British built an airfield on the south of the island, where many soldiers lost their lives.

Stiniva 8

One of the Adriatic's most celebrated coves **(right)**, Stiniva has a small shingle beach enclosed by curving rocky promontories. Some distance from the road, it can only be reached on foot or by mountain bike.

NEED TO KNOW

MAP B5 ■ Tourist Office: Šetalište Stare Isse 5, Vis town; 021 717 017; www. tz-vis.hr ■ Travel agencies include Alternatura (Komiža; 021 717 239; www.alternatura.hr); Ames Trips (Komiža; 091 390 3300; www.ames.hr); and Paiz (Vis town; 098 263 207)

King George III Fortress: open Jun–Sep: 10am–11pm daily; www.fortgeorge croatia.com

■ Trips to Biševo and the Blue Cave are organized by many businesses, such as Alternatura *(see left)*.

■ Located diagonally opposite the Vis town

ferry dock, Bejbi is a good spot for coffee or an evening drink.

■ The island is filled with military installations left by the British, Austrian and Yugoslav armed forces. Sign up for one of the military tours offered by local agents such as Alternatura or Paiz.

🔟 ⭐ Korčula Town

It's easy to see why the explorer Marco Polo would have been drawn to Korčula (even if it was not, as some suggest, his native town). There is no doubting the beauty of the place, a mosaic of terracotta rooftops encircled by medieval walls and punctuated by church spires, which juts out into the Adriatic and has the majestic Pelješac mountains as a backdrop. Evidence of former Venetian rule abounds, from the proud lions adorning its buildings to a cathedral dedicated to St Mark.

1 City Walls

Korčula's city walls **(below)** proved sturdy enough to see off an onslaught by the Ottoman Turks in 1571. In the 19th century, parts of the walls were taken down as they lost their defensive function. Only a few sections of the wall remain, including All Saints' Tower, which was one of the 12 original towers that formed part of the fortifications.

A scenic view of Korčula

MOREŠKA

Korčula is the only Dalmatian island where real swords are still used for dancing the Moreška (literally, "Moorish"). Dating from the 15th century, the dance has been performed in Korčula since the 16th century, and is believed to be a re-enactment of a battle between a Turkish king and a Moorish king. Today's simplified form sees the White King fight the Black King, to set his fiancée, captured by the Black King, free. When the White King triumphs, the maiden is liberated.

2 Collection of Icons

Situated in a hall owned by the All Saints Brotherhood, Korčula's oldest fraternity, this collection features objects used in ceremonies and processions as well as nine icons dating from the 14th–17th centuries, which were brought to Korčula from Crete.

3 Marco Polo Centre

This interpretation centre chronicles the life and travels of the medieval globetrotter, Marco Polo. It offers an insight into his connection with Korčula and the battle that took place near the island.

4 Town Hall

The 16th-century town hall **(right)** sits just inside the Land Gate. Its loggia recalls Korčula town's Venetian heritage.

Previous pages Sculpture of a lion on the Cathedral of St Domnius, Split

Map of Korčula Town

9 Land Gate and Steps

The sweep of steps up to the Land Gate provides a dramatic entrance to the Old Town. Set in a 14th-century bastion, the gate was once a crucial strongpoint on the walls.

10 Cathedral of St Mark

Completed in the 16th century, this cathedral **(below)** is one of the most charming eccle-siastical buildings in the Adriatic islands. The interior is a wonderful riot of both Gothic and Renaissance styles.

6 Town Museum

Opposite the cathedral is a small civic museum, which is set in the striking 16th-century Gabriellis Palace. Among the exhibits is a copy of a 4th-century Greek tablet.

7 Korčula Wooden Shipbuilding Exhibition

This exhibition in the town's small loggia explores the history of Korčula's wooden shipbuilding industry, with displays of tools and various ships.

5 Churches

Korčula town may be small, but it manages to cram in a wealth of churches. Look out for All Saint's Church, St Michael's, the Church of our Lady and St Peter's Church, which all stand within the Old Town walls.

8 Abbey Treasury

To the south of the cathedral stands the Abbey Treasury, with great works of art by Dubrovnik and Venetian artists, including masterpieces by Blaž Jurjev Trogiranin, Ivan Meštrović, Bassano and Carpaccio.

NEED TO KNOW

MAP E5 ■ Tourist Information: Trg 19. travnja 1921. br. 40; 020 715 701

Marco Polo Centre: Depolo; open Jun–Sep: 9am–9pm daily; Oct–May: hours vary, check website; www.gradskimuzej-korcula.hr; adm €8; children free

Town Museum: Trg Sv Marka; 020 711 420; open Jun–Sep:

10am–9pm Mon-Sat (to 3pm Sun); Oct–May: 10am–3pm Mon–Fri; adm €6; children free

Korčula Wooden Shipbuilding Exhibition: Ul. Korčulanskog statuta 1214; 020 716 529; open Jul & Aug: 9am–1pm & 6–9pm daily, Sep–Jun: by appt

Cathedral of St Mark and Abbey Treasury: Trg Sv Marka; 099 242 2133; open Apr & Oct: 9am–5pm

Mon–Sat; (May–Sep: to 7pm daily); Nov–Mar: by appt; adm €5, children €3

■ Housed in an old bastion, the popular bar Massimo *(see p82)* offers sweeping views out across the Pelješki Channel.

■ Visit on Mondays and Thursdays in high season to enjoy the Moreška *(see p63)*.

TOP 10 ⭐ Trogir

Trogir, a UNESCO World Heritage Site, is one of the most stunning places in the Mediterranean. Sitting on its own island with bridges linking it to the mainland on one side and Čiovo island on the other, the town forms a shimmering knot of orange roofs and traditional stone buildings, among which lies one of Croatia's most remarkable cathedrals. The well-preserved old centre is a pedestrianized oasis where the centuries peel back with every step.

1 Kamerlengo Fortress
This fortification **(below)** has guarded the western approaches to Trogir since the 15th century. Concerts and film screenings are held here in summer months.

2 Church of St John the Baptist
A small Romanesque church is all that remains of a great Benedictine monastery, the final resting-place of the Ćipiko family. Their tomb is decorated with a 15th-century relief of *The Mourning of Christ*.

3 Loggia and Clock Tower
Traditionally a place where criminals were tried, the 14th-century loggia is notable for the conspicuous gap on its eastern wall, when a Venetian stone lion was blown up by local activists in the 1930s.

4 Convent of St Nicholas
The art collection makes this modest convent worth visiting. The highlight, discovered in the 1920s, is the 3rd-or 4th-century Greek relief of Kairos. Also note the chests used by new arrivals to the convent.

5 Cathedral of St Lawrence
Highlights include the 13th-century portal or main entrance, lavishly adorned with biblical scenes carved by sculptor Radovan, and the Renaissance styling of the baptistry and St John's Chapel. Climb the tower **(left)** for views across Trogir and the surrounding coast.

6 Ćipiko Palace
This Gothic-Renaissance edifice is one of the town's most impressive palaces. It was once the base of the powerful 15th-century Ćipiko family.

THE LEGEND OF RAFIOLI

A speciality found across Trogir, *rafioli* is a short-bread cookie filled with ground almonds and orange and lemon zest. A popular local legend associated with it claims that a young girl, Rafioli, was once imprisoned in the Kamerlengo Tower. While waiting to be freed, she spent her days baking these delicious cookies. A nobleman from Trogir rescued her and brought her to his court, where she baked *rafioli* for him for the rest of her life.

7 Town Museum

Trogir's town museum is housed in the Garagnin-Fanfogna Palace and presents details of the town's eclectic past. It explores everything from the legacy left by the Greeks and Romans, to the flourishing of Trogir in the Middle Ages. The modern era is also explored via a series of objects that illustrate everyday life in the town.

Map of Trogir

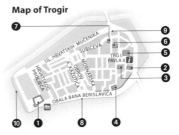

8 Riva

The waterfront Riva **(above)** is where locals and tourists come to wander or enjoy a meal or drink on balmy evenings. In season, boats line up here and visitors can book trips.

9 Land Gate

Part of the fortifications built by the Venetians, Land Gate is the most impressive of the surviving gates. A statue of St John, Trogir's patron saint, watches over new arrivals.

10 Marmont's Gloriette

During the Napoleonic era (1806–13) the governor of Napoleon's Illyrian Provinces, General Marmont, liked to recline here **(left)**, taking in the views. It is still a striking spot from which to relax and soak up the scenery.

NEED TO KNOW

MAP B3 ■ Tourist Information: Trg Ivana Pavla II 1; 021 885 628; www.visittrogir.hr

Kamerlengo Fortress: open Apr, Oct & Nov: 10am–6pm daily; May & Sep: 9am–8pm daily (Jun–Aug: to 10pm); adm €4

Church of St John the Baptist: Trg Ivana Pavla II; May–Sep: 9am–8pm Mon–Sat, noon–6pm Sun; Oct–Apr: by appt; adm €3

Convent of St Nicholas: Gradska 2; open Jul–Aug: 9am–1pm Mon–Sat; Sep–Jun: 10:30am–1pm & 3:30–5pm Mon–Sat; adm 5€

Cathedral of St Lawrence Bell Tower, Baptistry and Treasury: Trg Ivana Pavla II; 021 881 426; open times vary, call ahead; adm €3

Town Museum: Gradska vrata 4; 021 881 406; open times vary, call ahead; adm €4, children €3

■ The palm-fringed Riva is ideal for a relaxed coffee or meal. Try the Restoran Riva *(see p93)*, which is open all year.

■ Cross the bridge to the island of Čiovo for great views across to the Old Town.

🔟⭐ Diocletian's Palace, Split

Split's city centre is like no other in Europe. Built as a grand retirement home for Roman Emperor Diocletian, it later provided shelter for refugees from nearby Salona, who fled here in 615 CE when their own city was sacked. Today, the area occupied by the once mighty imperial palace – now a UNESCO World Heritage Site – is one of the best-preserved examples of late antiquity Roman architecture. With about 3,000 residents and crammed with bars and boutique art shops, the oldest core of Split buzzes with life all year round and offers a varied choice of things to see and do.

Peristyle ①
Once an antechamber to Diocletian's quarters, the dramatic, colonnaded square known as the Peristyle **(right)** is the heart of the palace complex.

EXPLORE SPLIT RESPONSIBLY

In 2023, Split introduced strict rules for visitors to curb behaviour that is considered inappropriate locally. Visitors should not consume alcohol within the historical centre or near schools; avoid consuming food and drink in public spaces; and do not stay in bars after working hours. Climbing and sitting on monuments is also forbidden, as is sleeping in public spaces. The measures are enforced by city order officers; breaching them will result in hefty fines.

Ethnographic ② Museum
Located in labyrinthine alleys south of the Vestibule, this museum includes folk costumes and incorporates the medieval Chapel of St Andrew, former site of Diocletian's bedchamber.

Cathedral of ④ St Domnius
Built over Diocletian's tomb, the main structure here **(below)** is Roman. Step inside to see the 13th-century pulpit, and a chapel and altar by sculptor Juraj Dalmatinac.

Subterranean ③ Chambers
The palace's underground vaults **(left)** mirror the layout of the imperial chambers that once stood above. They provide great insight into how the palace would have looked.

6 Bell Tower

The bell tower, which soars high above the magnificent cathedral, was completed in the early 20th century. The panoramic views of the city from the top **(left)** make the long climb worthwhile.

Plan of Diocletian's Palace

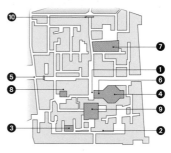

7 City Museum

East of the Peristyle, the City Museum is housed in the 15th-century Papalić Palace. As well as the artifacts relating to Split's history, the museum also houses the Emanuel Vidović Gallery.

8 Baptistry

An alley opposite the cathedral leads to the Bapistry, once the Roman Temple of Jupiter. Inside, a striking feature is the sculpture of John the Baptist by Croatian sculptor Ivan Meštrović (1883–1962).

9 Vestibule

Stone steps from the Peristyle lead to this domed area **(below)**, where guests used to wait to see the Emperor. At night, stars are visible through a gap in the top.

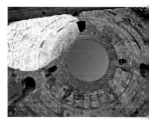

10 Golden Gate

This sturdy portal once led north to the nearby settlement of Salona. It has now been restored to its full splendour thanks to funding by a local bank.

5 Iron Gate

The western entrance to the palace, the Iron Gate, was altered in the medieval era when the 12th-century Church of Our Lady of the Belfry was built into its top storey. The belfry clock is thought to be the oldest surviving church tower on the Adriatic coast.

NEED TO KNOW

MAP M3 ▪ Tourist information: Peristyle; 021 345 606

Subterranean Chambers: open times vary, check website; www.mgs.hr; adm

Cathedral of St Domnius: Peristyle; 021 271 942; open 8am–8pm Mon–Sat, noon–6pm Sun; adm €5

Bell Tower: Peristyle; open 8am–8pm Mon–Sat, noon–6pm Sun; adm €7

City Museum: Papalićeva 1; 021 360 171; closed for renovation until further notice, call ahead for updates

▪ The spacious Luxor Café in the Peristyle is a good place to relax and refuel.

▪ Delve beyond the cupola to explore the upper tier of the palace. There are few major sights here, and the bars are a lot quieter than those below and offer breathtaking views of the Adriatic.

Other Sights in Split

Aerial view of Marjan Hill and the Split waterfront

1 Marjan Hill
MAP L5

From the west side of the town, steps lead up to this stretch of greenery, part of a protected nature reserve. The views from the top are spectacular, with the mountains stretching off towards Bosnia in the distance and large swathes of the Dalmatian coast and its islands visible on a clear day.

2 Riva
MAP L2

Split's palm-fringed, pedestrianized waterfront is where its citizens come to see and be seen. The many pavement cafés make this the perfect spot to relax and gaze seawards at the ferries as they slip off to the nearby islands.

3 Archeological Museum
The collections housed here (see p46) feature a variety of artifacts that date from Split's Roman, early Christian and medieval eras, as well as a few items dating from the time when Dalmatia was ruled by the Greeks.

Relief, Archeological Museum

4 Meštrović Gallery
The Croatian-born, Expressionist sculptor Ivan Meštrović (1883–1962) never realized his dream of retiring to this impressive building (see p46). Today it provides a fitting home for a fine collection of his work.

5 Gallery of Fine Arts
Housed in a beautifully restored 18th-century hospital, Split's main art gallery (see p46) holds one of the nation's best collections of Croatian art from the Renaissance onwards. It also hosts some ground-breaking contemporary shows.

6 Fish Market
MAP L2

This wonderfully pungent and colourful market bursts into life every morning of the week. Here you can feast your eyes on a rich spread of Adriatic seafood, accompanied by a cacophony of haggling buyers and sellers.

7 Bačvice
A short walk southeast from the centre of Split leads to this small bay (see p92), which shelters one of the city's most popular summer beaches. It is also home to a large waterfront entertainment centre filled with buzzing bars and nightclubs.

8 Trg Republike (Prokurative)
MAP L2

In contrast to the Roman parts of own, this square's grand architecture hints very clearly at Venetian origins.

9 Narodni Trg
MAP M2

When the Venetians rumbled into Split, they moved the focus of the city away from Diocletian's Palace, westwards and into this square. Highlights here are the 15th-century town hall and its grandiose ground-floor loggia.

10 Coastal Walk
MAP N6

The coastline stretching out from Bačvice is lined with beaches, cafés and nightclubs. East of here is a pretty coastal path leading past the tennis club where the 2001 Wimbledon champion Goran Ivanišević launched his career.

EMPEROR DIOCLETIAN

Emperor Diocletian

Diocletian grew up in a family of modest means in the Dalmatian town of Salona, before embarking on a meteoric rise through the military ranks of the Roman Empire to assume the top position. He demonstrated a taste for grand construction projects; his greatest legacy to Croatia is the lavish retirement palace that he built by the Adriatic, and was later to evolve into the city of Split. Retirement was an unconventional move for a Roman emperor – his predecessors had all died on the job. From his grand seaside residence, Diocletian looked on as the Empire began to crumble, and it was here that he eventually took his own life. Given Diocletian's notoriety as a persecutor of Christians, it is ironic that Split's cathedral was later built on the site of his tomb.

St George appears before Diocletian in this image from the late 13th-century manuscript *Scenes from the Life of St George.*

TOP 10 EVENTS IN DIOCLETIAN'S LIFE

1 245 CE: Diocletian is thought to have been born into a lowly Dalmatian family in Salona

2 282: Finds favour with Emperor Carus, and is made a Roman Count

3 283: Carus elevates his status to that of consul

4 284: Reaches his zenith, at the age of just 39, by becoming Roman Emperor

5 295: Commissions his seaside retirement palace in Split, which takes about a decade to complete

6 303: Outlaws Christianity, ordering the destruction of all churches and the persecution of Christians

7 305: Becomes the first Roman emperor to retire rather than die or be murdered on the job

8 308: Declines request to be reinstated as ruler of the Roman Empire

9 315: Diocletian's wife (Prisca) and daughter (Valeria) are murdered by Emperor Licinius

10 c 316: Poisons himself in his palace at Split

TOP 10 ⭐ Hvar

This island just about has it all, from the swanky bars and yacht berths of Hvar town to the UNESCO-protected agricultural land on the Stari Grad Plain. Despite its popularity, the island is by no means over-touristed. Its interior is filled with bucolic villages and vineyard-covered hills, and its coast has a plethora of empty bays and coves, especially towards the island's eastern tip. The restaurants offer a blend of modern and traditional fare, and there's a growing roster of good local wines.

PETAR HEKTOROVIĆ'S TVRDALJ

One of Stari Grad's most famous buildings is the Tvrdalj, which was built as a family villa by Renaissance poet Petar Hektorović (1487–1572) and intended to symbolize his humanistic outlook on life. The Tvrdalj also served as a fortified refuge for townsfolk in the event of attack. Self-sufficiency was ensured by a walled garden, a pigeon loft in the main tower and a saltwater pond full of mullet – features that still survive today.

Hvar Town 2
An attractive huddle of villas, bars and boutiques set around a steep-rimmed bay, Hvar town **(right)** is for many the epitome of Adriatic chic. Popular with both the yachting crowd and younger party goers, it is also oozing with culture, featuring a set-piece Renaissance square, a historic theatre and a clutch of monasteries.

3 Milna
Of the string of beach locations east of Hvar town, the largely modern Milna is the most popular. It is made up of rock and shingle beaches, and is well equipped with cafés and restaurants.

1 Hvar Fortress
Looking down on Hvar's port, this impressive fortress **(below)**, built in the 16th century, gives expansive views of the Pakleni islands. It's reached via an agave-lined zigzag walkway.

Pakleni Islands 4
Water taxis leave from Hvar to these islands just off the coast. The largest, Jerolim, Marinkovac and Sveti Klement, are popular for day trips due to their shingle beaches **(right)** and restaurants.

5 Vrboska
With buildings huddled on either side of an inlet spanned by a trio of bridges, Vrboska is famous for its traditional stone houses and the fortified, castle-like Church of St Mary, which rises above the village.

6 Jelsa
A fishing port based around a parish, Jelsa has excellent beaches and promenades. With a clutch of pleasant hotels and campsites, too, it's a popular family destination in summer. Jelsa is also famous for its wineries.

7 Sućuraj

This mellow port at the east of the island is the departure point for ferries to Drvenik on the mainland and provides access to some relatively uncommercialized coves and beaches.

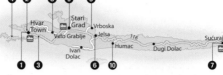

Map of Hvar Island

8 Velo Grablje

Set high in the hills between Hvar town and Stari Grad, Velo Grablje was the centre of the island's lavender-harvesting industry and remains a well-preserved example of a prosperous inland village, still complete with a village square, a church and traditional stone farmhouses.

9 Stari Grad

With its cobbled alleys, cute piazzas and colourful window-boxes, Stari Grad is one of the most soothing towns on the Adriatic coast. It is also one of the oldest towns in Europe. The UNESCO-protected Stari Grad Plain to the east of town still bears the pattern of field division that was adopted by Hvar's ancient Greek settlers.

10 Humac

Lying at the end of a winding road in the hills east of Jelsa, Humac is an atmospheric village of old houses and stone-paved streets, amid maquis and overgrown olive groves. The stalagmite- and stalactite-filled Grapčeva cave **(left)** is nearby.

NEED TO KNOW

MAP C4 ■ Tourist office (Hvar town): Trg svetog Stjepana 42; 021 741 059; www.visithvar.hr ■ Tourist office (Stari Grad): Obala dr. Franje Tuđmana 1; 021 765 763; www.visit-stari-grad.com

Hvar Fortress: open Apr & May: 9am–8pm daily; Jun–Sep: 8am–11pm daily

Tvrdalj, Stari Grad: open Jun & Sep: 10am–1pm; Jul & Aug: 10am–1pm & 5–8pm daily

■ Near Hvar town's catamaran dock, Sweet Republic *(see p82)* serves handmade vegan sweets, and is a quiet alternative to Riva cafés.

■ Car ferries run from Split to Stari Grad (three to six trips daily, depending on season) and from Drvenik to Sućuraj (five to ten times daily). Passenger-only catamarans run from Split to Hvar town twice a day during winter, as well as from Vis to Hvar town on Tuesdays, and from Dubrovnik between May and October.

■ If you're driving, arrive early at the ferry dock. Vehicles are loaded on a first-come, first-served basis. There are reservations on some car ferries running between Split and Stari Grad.

TOP 10 ⭐ Pelješac Peninsula

A long, bony limb of land stretching west from the mainland north of Dubrovnik, the Pelješac Peninsula includes much that is distinctive about Dalmatian life. The red wine here is celebrated as the best in the country, and restaurants offer many traditional specialities, from locally farmed oysters to meats baked slowly in charcoal-covered pots. While the main town Orebić offers well-equipped hotels, the tourist scene is mostly informal, with beachside campsites and bay-hugging villages adding to the appeal.

1 Mali Ston

This cluster of waterside houses **(left)** is famous for the oysters harvested in its enclosed, mainland-facing bay. A handful of excellent restaurants serve the local delicacy, drawing a year-round crowd of visiting gourmets.

2 Ston

Once a key fortress guarding the Republic of Ragusa's northern frontier, Ston stands at the western end of a stunning stretch of 14th-century walls. Running across the hillsides to link up with Mali Ston some 3 km (2 miles) away, the walls are open to visitors and offer sweeping views.

3 Orebić

This stately seaside town was famous for its 19th-century merchant fleet and still has the handsome villas and lush gardens **(right)** once owned by local ship captains. Orebić's long shingle beaches draw visitors from far and wide and Korčula town *(see p26)* is a short ferry ride across the Pelješki Channel.

4 Janjina

Occupying the high ground at Pelješac's narrowest point, Janjina offers a rare taste of rural Dalmatia. It is just a short walk downhill to the beaches of Drače, which face the mountainous mainland.

PELJEŠAC WINES

Croatia's finest red wines are grown on Pelješac's south-facing coast, where sunlight, arid soil and salty sea breezes combine to produce small but fully flavoured grapes. The most popular variety is Plavac Mali, an indigenous grape that is related to Zinfandel and produces a heady, velvety red. Dingač and Postup are the most famous wine-growing areas, and wine from either fetches a high price. All the local restaurants serve decent house wine, and there are plenty of specialist wineries offering the opportunity to taste and buy the best.

5 Dingač
Sheltering beneath craggy grey slopes, the wine-growing area of Dingač **(below)** is famous for the hillside-hugging vineyards that produce Croatia's best red wine. The grape harvest is notoriously difficult here due to the steep slopes.

Map of the Pelješac Peninsula

6 Trpanj
A quiet port backed by rugged mountains, Trpanj is the perfect base for exploring some of the off-the-beaten-track beaches of Pelješac's northern coast. Most celebrated of these is Divna, which lies at the end of a ravine to the west of town.

7 Kučište
A charming village featuring stone houses and small-boat piers sheltering beneath the slopes of Mount Sveti Ilija, Kučište is an ideal base for those who enjoy hill walking and mountain biking.

8 Žuljana
Squeezed into a south-facing cove at the end of a crooked ravine, the cute fishing village of Žuljana has one of Pelješac's finest shingle beaches. It is also a diver's paradise.

9 Viganj
The stiff breezes of the Pelješac Channel have helped Viganj become the prime windsurfing resort in Croatia **(right)**. Most of the surfers stay in one of Viganj's numerous campsites, and there is a fine shingle beach for those who prefer to take it easy and spend time lying in the sun.

10 Lovište
A quaint fishing village stretching along a broad shallow bay, Lovište is the perfect place to wind down and relax. Spend the day exploring the nearby beaches and smaller bays, or trying the fresh fish in the local restaurants.

NEED TO KNOW

MAP F5 ■ Tourist office: Trg Mimbeli, Orebić; 020 713 718; www.visitorebic-croatia.hr

Car hire and travel agent: Orebić Tours, Ulica Bana Jelačića 84, Orebić; 020 713 367; www.orebic-tours.hr

■ Café Croccantino, just around the corner from the Orebić ferry dock, is rightly celebrated for its ice cream and cakes – perfect for a quick treat before crossing the Channel to Korčula.

■ There is limited public transport on the peninsula, so you really need a car to explore. Hire one in Dubrovnik or from a local agent in Orebić.

The Top 10 of Everything

The idyllic bay at Milna, on the southwest coast of Hvar Island

TOP 10 Moments in History

1 4th Century BCE: Greeks and Illyrians in Dalmatia

Greek settlers began to cross the seas and join the Illyrian tribes who had already been eking out a living on the Dalmatian coastline. As the population along the coastal strip expanded, trade links and proto-settlements started to flourish.

2 1st Century CE: Romans Move into Dalmatia

The Roman Empire surged east, engulfing swathes of Croatia and snuffing out most of the Indigenous opposition. Wine production flourished as the conquerors brought their skills to a land whose soil and climate made it perfect for producing both red and white wines.

3 925 CE: Alleged First Croatian King Crowned

Croatia became a nation under King Tomislav, the "Father of the Croats", who united the country for the first time. Croatia's independence, however, was soon quashed by the power of the Huns and the mighty Venetian doges. The latter soon wielded greater influence over Dalmatia.

4 1409: Dalmatia Comes Under Venetian Control

King Ladislaus of Naples sold Dalmatia to the Venetian Republic for 100,000 ducats, but the Republic of Ragusa retained its independence from both Venice and the Ottoman Empire.

Statue of King Tomislav

5 1808: Napoleon Annexes Republic of Ragusa

In 1806, French troops saved the Republic of Ragusa from a month-long siege by Russian and Montenegrin forces. Two years later, Napoleon claimed Ragusa for France.

Portrait of Napoleon Bonaparte

6 1815: Dalmatia Comes Under Habsburg Rule

After a period of French rule, Ragusa and Dalmatia were awarded to the Habsburg Empire by the Congress of Vienna. Under Austrian rule, Dalmatia remained economically undeveloped, but tourism grew towards the end of the 19th century.

7 1918: First Yugoslav State Created in the Wake of World War I

With the fall of the Habsburg Empire at the end of World War I, Croatia voted to join the new Kingdom of Serbs, Croats and Slovenes (later renamed Yugoslavia). Croats expected a degree of national autonomy and were disap pointed when the union created a

Map of the 1918 Yugoslav state

Serb-dominated state centred on Belgrade. At this time, Ragusa officially became known as Dubrovnik.

(8) 1945: Tito Comes to Power

Croatian-born communist Josip Broz Tito built the Partisan movement in World War II and re-established Yugoslavia after the war. He created a federation in which Serbs, Croats, Slovenes, Montenegrins, Bosnians and Macedonians each had their own republic. Tito's Yugoslavia was thrown out of the Soviet bloc in 1948, improving relations with the West.

War after Croatian independence

(9) 1991: Croatia Declares its Independence

A landslide referendum saw Croatia gain independence from Yugoslavia. Irregular Serbian units, backed up by the Yugoslav military, attacked the republic and besieged Dubrovnik. Hostilities had ceased by the end of 1995, and all captured Croatian territory was returned by 1998.

(10) 2013–present: Croatia in Europe

Croatia joined the European Union in 2013. Ten years later, in 2023, the country adopted the euro and became part of the Schengen Zone.

TOP 10 HISTORICAL FIGURES

1 Emperor Diocletian
Diocletian (245–316) built a retirement palace on the Adriatic coast, founding Split in the process *(see p30)*.

2 King Tomislav
Allegedly crowned in c 925, Tomislav was one of the first rulers to unite Adriatic and inland Croatia in the same state.

3 Grgur of Nin
This 10th-century bishop campaigned for the use of the Croatian language (rather than Latin) in church services.

4 Faust Vrančić
Dubbed as the "Croatian Leonardo da Vinci", this talented inventor and linguist (1551–1617) created the first Croatian dictionary.

5 Nikola Tesla
Tesla (1856–1943) was one of the most gifted inventors of modern times. He is best known for his contributions in the field of alternating current.

6 Ante Pavelić
Fascist leader Pavelić (1889–1959) served as puppet ruler of Axis-occupied Croatia from 1941 to 1945. His rule provoked one of Europe's biggest anti-fascist uprisings.

7 Marshal Josip Broz Tito
Tito (1892–1980) fought the Axis forces before leading Yugoslavia after World War II.

8 Anka Berus
Croatia's first female minister, Berus (1903–1991) is widely admired for her efforts to secure workers' rights.

9 Franjo Tuđman
Tuđman (1922–99) became the first president of the newly independent Croatia in 1991.

10 Vesna Parun
Parun (1922–2010) was one of the greatest Croatian poets of the 20th century.

Franjo Tuđman

TOP10 Old Towns

A corner of magical Trogir

1 Trogir
Set picturesquely on an islet between the mainland and the island of Čiovo, Trogir *(see pp28–9)* can make a credible claim for the title of finest old town on the Adriatic coast. Trogir's unity of design makes it special, which is why the locals call it the "town museum".

2 Stari Grad (Hvar)
Stari Grad – literally "Old Town" – is a fitting name for this settlement *(see p77)* founded by Greeks in 384 BCE. Central Stari Grad's narrow alleys have an air of antiquity, although most of the stone houses date from medieval or Renaissance times. The fortified Tvrdalj, or villa, of poet Petar Hektorović offers an insight into the lifestyles of 16th-century Hvar nobles.

3 Dubrovnik
Lord Byron's "Pearl of the Adriatic" is Croatia's most famous set-piece. Encapsulated within the hulking medieval walls is a perfectly preserved Baroque city-state *(see pp12–19)*, sandwiched between a sweep of limestone mountains to the north and the Adriatic to the south. Highly popular with tourists, the Old City *(see pp66–75)* can often get crowded in summer, but there's no doubting its allure.

4 Hvar Town
It is easy to see why Hvar town *(see p77)* is the summer getaway of choice for Croatia's city dwellers. The charming old core, crammed with Venetian architecture, sweeps around a wide Adriatic bay. High above, a rambling fort watches over the summer scene of pavement

Hvar town's bustling harbour in summer

cafés, fish restaurants and bobbing tour boats. The main square is dominated by the contours of the Cathedral of St Stephen (see p45).

5 Split

No staid museum piece, Split's Old Town (see pp30–33) is a living and breathing slice of history, formed around the confines of the Emperor Diocletian's palatial waterfront retirement home, and adapted over the centuries by Split citizens.

6 Kut (Vis)

Relatively few visitors have discovered the historic Kut district of Vis town (see p22), with its outstanding Renaissance triple-naved church, Our Lady of Spilica, its swathe of old Venetian merchant dwellings, and its trio of first-rate restaurants – Pojoda (see p56), Vatrica and Val. These gastronomic institutions serve dishes prepared using local ingredients, grown in Vis's unique microclimate, fertile fields and rich fishing grounds.

7 Komiža (Vis)

Set around a bay on the western shores of Vis, Komiža (see p79) is a medieval fishing port that has changed little through the centuries. Stout houses adorned with family crests huddle around narrow streets and tiny piazzas, while a spectacular pair of sumptuously decorated churches are testament to Komiža's erstwhile wealth as the centre of the Adriatic anchovy-processing business.

8 Ston

The historic salt-manufacturing town of Ston (see p95) was bought by the Republic of Ragusa in 1335, becoming a key fortress on the northern border of the republic. The town walls, running from Ston to the port of Mali Ston, 3 km (2 miles) east, are among the best preserved in mainland Europe. The uniform grid pattern of the town attests to the order and proportion for which Ragusa's urban planners were once famed.

9 Lastovo Town
MAP D6

Unusually, Lastovo town (see p97) turns its back on the Adriatic and tumbles in the opposite direction. Less ornate than many other Dalmatian towns, its most striking buildings are a group of 20 or so Renaissance stone houses, characterized by their terraces and chimneys.

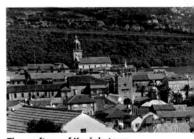

The rooftops of Korčula town

10 Korčula Town

Surrounded by walls, Korčula is the best-preserved medieval island town in the Adriatic. Enjoying its own rocky promontory, this old town (see pp26–7), carved over the centuries by the Venetians, still feels like an oasis not yet well acquainted with the 20th century, let alone the 21st. Within its walls lie churches, seafood restaurants, and the site where, locals believe, their most famous inhabitant, Marco Polo, was born.

TOP 10 Cathedrals and Churches

The Church of Our Lady of the Rocks, situated on the island of Lopud

1 Our Lady of the Rocks, Lopud

MAP G6

Some of the Dubrovnik region's best Renaissance artworks are inside this parish church on a promontory above the ferry dock. Overlooking the altar is a three-panel *Virgin and Child* painting by Dubrovnik master Nikola Božidarević. The altar screen is a masterpiece of stone carving.

2 Cathedral of St Mark, Korčula

An outstanding example of late medieval architecture, Korčula's Cathedral of St Mark *(see p27)* dominates the Old Town from the peninsula's highest point. Its distinctive tower is topped by an octagonal cupola; below, the façade

has late Gothic details, notably Adam and Eve squatting over the main door. The interior features a splendid altar painting by Tintoretto of saints Mark, Bartholomew and Jerome.

3 Our Lady of the Pirates, Komiža

MAP B5

Perched serenely above the main family beach at the northern end of Komiža's waterfront, this is one of Dalmatia's most unusual churches. It has three naves of almost equal size, each with its own high altar. Legend has it that a painting of the Virgin was stolen from the church by pirates, only to return washed up on the beach when the thieves were shipwrecked in a divine storm.

4 Our Lady of the Snows, Cavtat

MAP H7

Another church with an unusual name – referring to a miraculous snow storm that occurred early one August – this former monastery church stands at the end of Cavtat's palm-fringed harbour. Inside, Božidar Vlatković's *Virgin and Child* (1494) hangs above the main altar, while a Viktor

Dobričević polyptych at the back of the church portrays saints Michael, Nicholas and John the Baptist. The church is the focus of festivities on 5 August, with religious processions involving the whole town.

5 Dubrovnik Cathedral

Legend has it that Dubrovnik Cathedral *(see pp66–7)* was founded by Richard the Lionheart in gratitude for his life being spared during a violent storm that washed him up on the island of Lokrum. One of the country's most striking religious buildings, its treasures include Baroque frescoes, the Byzantine skull case of St Blaise and *Ascension* by Titian.

Statue at the Church of St Blaise, Dubrovnik

6 Cathedral of St Lawrence, Trogir

The 13th-century west portal by local master Radovan is the *pièce de résistance* of this remarkable cathedral *(see pp28–9)*. Look out for the figures of Adam and Eve on either side, standing proudly over a pair of Venetian lions (indicating the influence Venice once had over Trogir). Arranged around the upper sections of the portal are depictions of the saints and scenes of local life.

Cathedral of St Lawrence, Trogir

7 Church of St Blaise, Dubrovnik

Dubrovnik's revered patron saint, St Blaise *(see p15)*, is said to have saved the city from sacking by the Venetians. He pops up throughout the city but is perhaps most pleasingly represented in this 18th-century church.

8 Orthodox Church, Dubrovnik
MAP F9

Dubrovnik has been home to an Orthodox Christian community for many centuries, and this is their main place of worship in the Old City. Set behind wrought-iron railings, the church was built in Neo-Romanesque style with Byzantine and Moorish elements, and has squat rectangular belfries protruding from its ornate façade. Inside, a carved wooden icon screen is studded with portraits of saints. The church's collection of medieval icons, prayer books, and 19th- and 20th- century portraits by local painter Vlaho Bukovac is housed in a small museum next door.

9 Cathedral of St Stephen, Hvar Town
MAP C4

This 16th-century Renaissance building stands on the site of an old Benedictine monastery. One highlight is the altar's understated 13th-century *Madonna and Child*.

10 Mušter, Komiža
MAP B5

Set amid vines on a steep bluff overlooking the fishing town of Komiža, the Mušter is a fortified former monastery with jutting bastions and a stout defensive tower, which was built by the Benedictines. The monastery church, dedicated to fisher's patron St Nicholas, contains Baroque altars and an old organ.

TOP 10 Museums and Galleries

1 Gallery of Fine Arts, Split

MAP N1 ■ Ulica kralja Tomislava 15 ■ 021 350 110 ■ Open 10am–6pm Tue–Sun (to 9pm Thu) ■ Adm ■ www.galum.hr

This major collection covers Croatian art through the ages. Look out for masterful portraits by Vlaho Bukovac (1855–1922) and moody cityscapes by Emanuel Vidović (1870–1953).

Gallery of Fine Arts, Split

2 Archaeological Collection Issa, Vis Town

MAP B5 ■ Viški boj 12 ■ 021 329 340 ■ Closed for renovation, call ahead for updates ■ Adm

Sculptures, weapons and everyday items illuminate life in the Ancient Greek town of Issa (modern Vis town).

3 The Island of Brač Museum, Škrip

MAP C3 ■ 091 637 0920 ■ Open 9am–7pm Mon–Sat, 10am–1pm & 3–7pm Sun ■ Adm

Treasures from all over Brač are housed in the Radojković Tower, which shows traces of Illyrian, Roman and early Croatian architecture.

4 Archaeological Museum, Split

MAP M5 ■ Zrinsko-Frankopanska 25 ■ 021 329 340 ■ Open Jun–Sep: 9am–2pm & 3–8pm Mon–Sat; Oct–May: 10am–2pm & 3–8pm Mon–Fri, 9am–2pm Sat ■ Adm

Exhibits at this museum include Ancient Greek ceramics, weaponry from the 6th to 9th centuries, over 70,000 coins, and amphorae recovered from shipwrecks.

5 Branislav Dešković Gallery, Bol

MAP C4 ■ Porat bolskih pomoraca 7 ■ 091 635 2700 ■ Open Jul & Aug: 9am–2pm & 5–10pm Tue–Sun (Sep–Jun: to 3pm Tue–Sat) ■ Adm ■ www.czk-brac.hr

This small gallery on the Adriatic coast displays local artists, as well as those from other parts of Croatia. Of particular interest is the career-spanning collection of works by Expressionist Ignjat Job (1895–1936).

6 Maritime Museum, Dubrovnik

Explore the Maritime Museum's intriguing collection (see p13) spotlighting Dubrovnik's merchant marine dominance in the leading Mediterranean fleets between the 16th and 18th centuries.

7 Meštrović Gallery, Split

MAP L6 ■ Šetalište Ivana Meštrovića 46 ■ 021 340 800 ■ Open May–Oct: 9am–7pm Tue–Sun (Nov–Apr: to 5pm) ■ Adm

Many of Ivan Meštrović's sculptures, including a huge *Pietà* and bronze, marble, plaster and wood works, can be viewed at his former summer residence. Explore the garden, where wide-reaching sea views complement bronze sculptures by the artist.

Meštrović Gallery, Split

Exterior of the Hermitage of Blaca

⑧ Hermitage of Blaca, Brač

MAP C4

This 16th-century monastery and its contents, including correspondence between the last priest and the Royal Astronomical Society in London, have been frozen in time since 1963. A stunning location and roaming goats enhance its appeal. Access is on foot.

⑨ Kuća Bukovac, Cavtat

MAP H7 ▪ Bukovčeva 5 ▪ 020 478 646 ▪ Open Apr–Oct: 9am–7pm Mon–Sat (to 2pm Sun); Nov–Mar: 9am–6pm Tue–Sat (to 1pm Sun) ▪ Adm

The Croatian painter Vlaho Bukovac was born in this house in 1855. Today, it retains the qualities of a typical 19th-century bourgeois home. It is now a museum dedicated to Bukovac.

⑩ Stari Grad Museum, Stari Grad

MAP C4 ▪ Ulica braće Biankini 4 ▪ 021 766 324 ▪ Open Jul & Aug: 10am–1pm & 7–9pm Mon–Sat, 7–9pm Sun; May, Jun, Sep & Oct: 10am–1pm Mon–Sat ▪ Adm

This museum is worth visiting for the building alone – a villa with many Neo-Renaissance features intact. Works by local artists Bartul Petrić (1899–1974), Juraj Plančić (1899–1930), Pavo Dulčić (1947–1974) and Magda Dulčić (1965–2016) take up a whole floor. There is an archaeological collection too.

TOP 10 PUBLIC MONUMENTS

1 Orson Welles, Split
The Hollywood actor-director spent a lot of time in Split, a connection honoured by the monument sculpted by his Croatia-born partner Oja Kodar.

2 Father Andrija Kačić Miošić, Makarska
An impressive tribute to this 18th-century priest and poet.

3 Marko Marulić, Split
Meštrović's homage to the Split-born writer (1450–1524) often dubbed "the father of Croatian Literature".

4 Monument to a Tourist, Makarska
This seafront sculpture shows a "seagull" (a nickname given to Dalmatian men who enjoy romancing women, especially tourists) hugging a girl.

5 Orlando's Column, Dubrovnik
Standard-bearer for the Divine Republic, Orlando flies the Libertas flag of the Dubrovnik Festival in summer *(see p14)*.

6 Ivan Gundulić, Dubrovnik
Oversized Meštrović statue, honouring this local 17th-century poet.

7 Dr Franjo Tuđman, Split
Croatia's first president is shown in a thoughtful pose in a dignified statue at the entrance to Split harbour.

8 Nikola Duboković, Jelsa, Hvar
Cast by the great Ivan Rendić, this monument to a local seafarer is one of Dalmatia's finest public sculptures.

9 The New Riva, Split
The westward extension of Riva has metal plaques that mark the achievements of local sportspeople.

10 Grgur Ninski, Split
A colossal image of Gregory of Nin, who campaigned for Mass to be conducted in Old Church Slavonic.

Statue of Grgur Ninski in Split

🔟 Beaches

golf-cart taxi for a small fee. A lively bar at the back of the beach provides refreshments.

3 Zlatni Rat, Brač
MAP C4

Lapped by the currents of the Adriatic, the "Golden Cape" – a popular sweep of fine shingle that curls out from the pine-fringed southern flank of the island of Brač – is much eulogized. Photos of this distinctive landmark near the resort of Bol are, rightly, omnipresent in holiday brochures.

1 Banje Beach, Dubrovnik
MAP K9

The sand may be imported, and there's an entry charge to the section with sun loungers, but the sweeping views of old Dubrovnik and the island of Lokrum are hard to beat, and the waters are exceptionally clean.

Banje beach, Dubrovnik

2 Šunj, Lopud

A bay-enclosed crescent of fine shingle at the eastern end of Lopud island, Šunj (see p99) is one of the finest beaches in the Dubrovnik region, but it is rarely overcrowded due to its island location. The 40-minute walk from the Lopud ferry dock takes you through a wonderful Mediterranean landscape of olive groves, drystone walls and maquis. If you don't feel like walking, take a

4 Kamenice, Komiža, Vis
MAP B5

There are several pebbly coves immediately south of Komiža, and Kamenice is the largest and best equipped. It spreads beneath a sandy bluff covered with agaves and other Mediterranean flora. Kamenice's beach bar is a party destination that draws a young crowd on summer nights. The dog-friendly smaller bay just north of Kamenice is ideal for those with a canine companion.

5 Milna, Hvar
MAP C4

Even though there are several beaches in Hvar Town, many visitors make their way to Milna, which is 5 km (3 miles) east. Stone slabs and rocks abut the sea at the centre of the village, and there's a fine shingle beach a short walk to the west. There are several good restaurants above the beaches, and Milna offers plenty of parking space.

6 Trstenica, Orebić

You couldn't wish for a more spectacular location to unfurl your towel than Trstenica beach (see p99), with its collage of fine shingle and sand. Looking across

Trstenica beach, Orebić

the water, to the nearby island of Korčula, you can see the terracotta roof tiles of Korčula town, encircled by evocative starched mountain-scapes – a stunning view.

7 Pržina Bay, Lumbarda
MAP E5

While chocolate-box beauty Korčula town gets all the plaudits, the nearby town of Lumbarda has much better beaches. Pržina Bay has a decent sandy beach with a sprinkling of cafés in a very low-key scene. Buses run daily from Korčula town, while in summer there are boats as well. If Pržina Bay gets a little too crowded for your liking, nearby Bilin Žal tends to be a bit quieter.

8 Proizd, Vela Luka, Korčula
MAP C5

Bathing spots don't get much more dramatic than Proizd, a rocky island just off the western coast of Korčula, accessible by a water taxi from Vela Luka. Proizd's popularity rests on the huge slabs of rock that slope steeply into clear seas on its northern side, providing perfect perches on which to catch the sun's rays. A restaurant and café are also close at hand.

9 Gradac

The small town of Gradac (see p88) has the longest beach in Croatia, and the best on the Makarska Riviera. Shingle and pebbles abound along the tree-fringed shoreline. Out to sea, the island of Hvar looms on the horizon. Some sections of the beach offer tourist facilities, others are far more rustic. In summer it can be tricky to find a secluded spot.

10 Pakleni Islands
MAP B4–C4

This necklace of tiny islands just off Hvar is defined by its beaches and waterfront position. In fact, the name Pakleni derives from the pine resin, *paklina*, once used to waterproof boats. The islands are only a short boat trip from Hvar town, but the beaches here are different from those of their neighbour. Here, there is little in the way of tourist development to spoil the picturesque Adriatic setting.

A beach on the Pakleni Islands

TOP10 Sailing Routes

The beautiful waters between Dubrovnik and Korčula

1 Dubrovnik–Korčula

This southern-Adriatic route eases its way from Dubrovnik *(see pp66–75)* to Koločep, Lopud, Šipan and Mljet *(see p97)*. From the Mljet National Park, head up the Pelješki Channel en route to Korčula town *(see pp26–7)*. A detour from Šipan to Ston, from where you can walk to Mali Ston *(see p96)* and savour Adriatic fish, is well worth it.

2 Split–Dugi Otok

This stunning but less well-trodden route takes sailors from Split *(see pp30–33)* to Šolta *(see p79)*, Rogoznica and Žirje, then into the Kornati Islands archipelago, where Piškera has a good marina. From here, journey to Dugi Otok before returning via Primošten, which has become quite a hub for sailors over the years.

3 Trogir–Lastovo

Watch enviously from Trogir marina *(see pp28–9)* as the millionaires moor up on the Riva before heading due south to Brač *(see pp78–9)*, Hvar *(see pp34–5)*, Korčula *(see pp26–7)* and Lastovo *(see p97)*. For a real Robinson Crusoe experience, explore the islets to the northeast – Češvinica, Kručica, Stomorina and Saplun. Saplun has the added bonus of sand beaches.

4 Vis–Korčula, via Hvar

The direct route from Vis to Korčula runs through open sea; it's far more interesting to take this two-to three-day detour via Hvar town, the mysterious southern coast of Hvar island, and the beautiful uninhabited Šćedro island.

5 Split–Vis

Many yachts make a beeline for Brač and Hvar, and miss out on the beauty of Šolta (much favoured by the Splićani) and Vis. Hvar certainly has its attractions, though – not least of which are the plentiful secluded coves that are flanked by impressive mountains.

6 Bays and Beaches of Pelješac and Korčula

Start and finish in Korčula by taking this three-day circuit of southern Dalmatia's best beaches, working your way around the south of Korčula

Aerial view of the Pelješac beach

a Bačva Bay and Pupnatska Luka,
eturning by way of the southern
oast of Pelješac.

7 Vis to the Outer Islands

omiža is a good starting point for
two- to three-day tour of Croatia's
vesternmost islands. The grey volcanic
one of Jabuka and lighthouse-topped
dge of Palagruža are particularly
luring, while the nearest island to
omiža, Biševo, has fine beaches
nd some seasonal taverns.

8 Trogir–Dubrovnik

Be warned: this is a trip for
erious sailing enthusiasts, with big
stances between stops. Starting
om Trogir, the route takes in
var, Vis, Vela Luka (Korčula),
lljet and Dubrovnik

he Riva at Trogir

9 Split–Dubrovnik

An extended one-way charter
lows a thorough exploration of
entral and southern Dalmatia,
king in Split, Trogir, Šolta, Brač,
var, Vis, Korčula, Mljet and
ubrovnik. Take the time to explore
lands and islets, such as Pakleni
toci (see p49) and the islands
round Mljet's Polače Bay. This route
so allows an exploration of more
an one settlement on each island.

10 Trogir–Trogir

A two- to three-day trip out
Trogir takes you to the semi-wild
eaches of Drvenik Mali and Veli, and
e alluring Šešula inlet on the west-
n flanks of Šolta, before returning
a the eastern coast of Čiovo.

TOP 10 Outdoor Activities

Windsurfing off the Dalmatian coast

1 Windsurfing
Big Blue Sport: www.bigblue sport.com

Windswept coastlines on Brač and along the Pelješki Channel (Korčula and Pelješac) are all popular haunts for windsurfers.

2 Rafting
Rafting Experience Cetina: www.raftingexperiencecetina.hr

Adrenaline-fuelled white-water rafting trips are becoming increasingly popular, with a number of operators organizing trips on the Cetina river. Trips generally last from 3 to 4 hours, and take place on the lower stretch of this 105-km- (65-mile-) long waterway, around 20 minutes from the coastal town of Omiš (see p89).

3 Walking and Hiking
Headwater: www.head water.com

Dalmatia has an almost infinite number of walking and hiking opportunities, from easy, low-level walks to steep ascents requiring a higher level of fitness. Seek local advice and ensure that you have the right equipment. UK-based Headwater organize walking holidays around the Dalmatian coast.

4 Tennis
National heroes Goran Ivanišević, Iva Majoli, Mario Ančić and Marin Čilić have all fuelled Croatia's love of tennis. Public court can be found near resort hotels and towns throughout Dalmatia. One of the region's most famous courts is in Bačvice (see p32), Split, where Ivanišević trained as a youngster.

5 Scuba Diving
Croatian Diving Federation: www.diving-hrs.hr

Dive schools along the Dalmatian coast offer trial dives, diving courses, equipment hire, night dives and wreck dives. Some of the best diving can be done with Biševo's Blue Cave from the island of Vis, where there are myriad offshore wrecks. Contact the Croatian Diving Federation for more information.

6 Climbing
The vaulting peaks of the Biokovo mountain ranges have an irresistible allure to mountaineers, who flock here from all over Europe. There are also numerous climbing routes on the cliffs and canyons surrounding Split. Organized tours with qualified instructors advise climbers of all abilities.

Rock climbing near Split

7 Swimming

Given Croatia's lengthy coastline, it's hardly surprising that swimming is a popular outdoor sport. Those not keen to swim in the sea will find enclosed pools near the waterfronts in Korčula, Split and many other towns.

8 Sea Kayaking

Dalmatia's craggy coastline and many islands make it the perfect place to try sea kayaking. The majority of trips are centred around Dubrovnik and the Elafiti Islands. You can take anything from a short excursion to a week-long break. Local travel agencies in Dubrovnik can organize sea-kayaking tours.

Sea kayaking by Dubrovnik Old City

9 Snorkelling

Exploring the waters is cheap and easy: just don a mask and flippers, and you're away.

10 Picigin, Split

A summer sport peculiar to Split, picigin is more about posing than point-scoring. Head to Bačvice *(see p32)*, stand in the sea with a small black rubber ball, wearing your best swim-wear and designer sunglasses, throw the ball nonchalantly then catch it with one hand, and you will blend in perfectly with the Splićani.

TOP 10 SPECTATOR SPORTS

An Italy–Croatia football match

1 Football
Dalmatians are passionate about football. Football shirts and the graffiti of their fans (known as the Torcida) attest to the fact that most support premier-division Hajduk Split.

2 Basketball
Dalmatia's most famous stars, Dražen Petrović (1964–1993) and Krešimir Ćosić (1948–1995), fuelled the nation's dedication to the sport.

3 Tennis
Croatians support their home-grown tennis talent with as much energy as they use to play the game.

4 Sailing
Regular regattas and boat shows have made sailing more than just a leisure activity.

5 Beach Volleyball
In peak season, beach volleyball matches spring up along the Makarska Riviera.

6 Water Polo
A strong national team has secured water polo a sizable following.

7 Athletics
Split-born Blanka Vlašić is a two-time world champion in high jump and has two Olympic medals – silver and bronze.

8 Cycling
Brač hosts the Uvati Vitar, a three-day bike marathon in May. The Tour of Croatia, a popular men's cycling race, has one of its stages in Dalmatia.

9 Handball
Handball surged in popularity when Croatia won gold at the 2004 Olympics.

10 Rowing
The Skelin brothers from Split took silver at the 2004 Olympics. Most Dalmatian towns have a rowing club.

🔟 Children's Dalmatia

Exploring the city walls in Dubrovnik is a great family day out

1 Fortifications and Towers

Dalmatia overflows with towers and fortifications offering stunning views. Lather on the sunscreen and carry plenty of water. Cafés located along the way help ease the strain for kids, often offering high vantage points at the top of towers and in the fortifications themselves.

2 Aquaparks

An increasingly common feature of Dalmatia's beach resorts is the aquapark made up of inflatable blocks, ramps and walkways, allowing children to slide and splash around in shallow waters under the watchful eye of supervisors. There's usually an entrance fee, and lifebelts are provided. Well-equipped aquaparks can be found at Bol (see p78) and at Soline beach, near Vrboska (see p80).

3 Outdoor Cinemas

This traditional feature of Dalmatian life is once again a cultural mainstay, with the renovation of seaside cinemas. As well as offering fresh maritime breezes, al fresco screens in Dubrovnik, Bol, Supetar, Split, Vis, Hvar, and some other towns offer up-to-date choice of movies including options for family and children, which usually start early in the evening.

4 Public Swimming Pools

They may not be plush, but Dalmatia has some of the best-located public swimming pools in Europe, allowing parents to enjoy views of places such as Korčula Old Town, the island of Šolta (from Split) and the bay at Šibenik while the kids take a dip.

5 Playparks

Every Dalmatian town has a traditional playpark with swings, slides and climbing frames. Among the best equipped are those behind the main beach in Makarska (see p87) and on the south side of Gruž harbour in Dubrovnik.

6 Adventure Sports

If your older children crave a little excitement, adrenaline-pumping white-water rafting, sea

River rafting on the Cetina river

kayaking, river canoeing, sailing, mountain biking and organized hiking trips can be arranged at local travel agencies.

7 Ferries
The whole length of the Dalmatian coast is awash with catamarans and ferries of all shapes and sizes, transforming a sightseeing visit to an island into a sea-borne adventure. It's best to leave the car behind at the height of the summer.

8 Resort Hotels
The swimming pools, tennis courts and other leisure facilities at resort-style hotels will keep kids happily occupied for hours. Full- and half-board options are worth considering, particularly with younger children.

Child-friendly Amfora Resort, Hvar

9 Cycling
Once you get away from the busy highways and tourist resorts Dalmatia is replete with cycling opportunities. Many hotels and camp-sites provide or rent bikes to guests. Bicycle seats for young children are almost always available.

10 Beaches
Sandy beaches may be few and far between, but Dalmatia has long stretches of clean, sun-kissed pebble and shingle beach. Even at the height of summer, you will find whole swathes of shoreline deserted. On busy public beaches, snack bars, sun loungers and parasols are common – some have changing rooms and showers.

TOP 10 CHILDREN'S ATTRACTIONS

Windsurfing at Zlatni Rat Beach

1 Zlatni Rat, Bol
This is one of Dalmatia's best family beaches, with windsurfing, kayaking and an inflatable aquapark nearby.

2 Croatia's "Dead Sea" Lake
Children are delighted to find they can float with ease in the salt waters of the Mrtvo More, a sea-fed lake on the island of Lokrum *(see p20)*.

3 Biševo's Blue Cave
On a sunny day, children will find this spot mesmerizing *(see p23)*.

4 Beach Activities, Hvar
The beach just outside the Amfora Resort is a good place to hire snorkelling equipment and mountain bikes.

5 Spanish Fort, Hvar Town
This 16th-century fort is a firm favourite with all ages, and the young ones can burn off some energy on the steep ascent.

6 Žnjan, Split
This large pebble beach, 4 km (2 miles) east of central Split, is well equipped with trampolines and playparks.

7 Bačvice Beach, Split
The sandy bottom of Bačvice Bay is famously shallow, making it perfect for safe paddling and playing.

8 Banje Beach, Dubrovnik
The banana boat rides are popular with older kids in summer *(see p48)*.

9 Klis Fortress
This grizzled medieval fortress *(see p88)* situated above the village of the same name will fire the imagination.

10 Sokol grad Fortress
The dramatic location of this clifftop castle is as stirring as they come; and there's an audiovisual display inside.

🔟 Restaurants

Sashimi at Bugenvila, Cavtat

1 Bugenvila, Cavtat
A beautiful location, smooth service and plenty of imagination in the kitchen make this one of the best places to eat (see p101) in Southern Dalmatia. Only freshly sourced food is served, and the menu changes accordingly. Excellent cocktails, too.

2 Pojoda, Vis Town
A superb seafood restaurant (see p83), Pojoda is famed for serving many of the old island recipes that have been forgotten elsewhere, with barley and chickpeas featuring alongside quality fish and lobster.

3 Vila Koruna, Mali Ston
Dine on oysters and mussels plucked straight from the waters in front of the restaurant (see p101). The food is spiced with *fleur de sel* (flower of salt) from the salt plain in Ston, the oldest active saltworks in the world. The restaurant is equally adept at conjuring up creative dishes with fish and shellfish.

4 Bakus, Ston
Ston is considered the oyster capital of Southern Dalmatia, but Bakus (see p101) serves much more besides, with locally caught fish and home-grown vegetables drawing locals and visiting gourmets alike. The seafood pasta dishes are outstanding, but leave room for a dessert.

5 Giaxa, Hvar Town
A gourmet favourite, Giaxa (see p83) serves locally sourced fish, seafood and vegetable dishes in an elegant 15th-century palace. Booking in advance is recommended, especially in the summer.

6 Jastožera, Komiža
The fishing port of Komiža is famous for its lobster, and Jastožera (see p83) is the best place to eat it. The name itself means "The Lobster Pen", and the tables are set around a large stone tank in which the freshly caught specimens are kept, before being served in many ways. The fish here is also first class.

7 Noštromo, Split
This is the best place to eat (see p93) in the centre of town. It is just by the fish market, so the seafood is about as fresh as it gets. The decor is light and airy – a refreshing change from nautical theming.

8 Nautika, Dubrovnik
Long the most famous restaurant in the city, Nautika (see p75) has many would-be detractors, but it usually hits the spot for most diners. The menu nods towards the Adriatic with locally sourced fish, but there are also meat and

Nautika, Dubrovnik

vegetarian dishes. Vying for centre stage, though, are the wonderful views of the Old City to one side and Lovrijenac Fortress to the other from the lovely terrace.

9 Adio Mare, Korčula Town

This bustling seafood restaurant (see p83), awarded two toques by Gault & Millau in 2018 and 2019, is located in the old quarter of Korčula town, close to the reputed birthplace of Marco Polo. Fragrant smoke billows from the fish grill, beckoning in the crowds – but despite the volume of diners, the restaurant manages to maintain great quality, and few leave unsatisfied.

The busy dining area at Adio Mare in Korčula town

10 Orsan, Dubrovnik

Local foodies flock to this restaurant in Dubrovnik's Old City (see p75) for classic Dalmatian seafood dishes and a stunning view away from the crowds. The menu includes octopus salad, black risotto (prepared with cuttlefish ink), freshly caught fish and a limited selection of meat dishes. The best tables are pine-tree-shaded and perched right by the water's edge, along the quay of the Orsan Yacht Club marina.

TOP 10 CULINARY HIGHLIGHTS

Local shrimp – a popular choice

1 Shrimp (Buzara)
This rich and flavoursome seafood dish is a Dalmatian speciality. Shrimp are gently simmered in a sauce of tomato, onion and herbs.

2 Ston Oysters (Oštrige)
Head to Mali Ston for divine oysters, plucked from the beds just offshore.

3 Pag Cheese (Paški Sir)
Pag produces a distinctive salted sheep's cheese – the finest cheese in the country.

4 Black Risotto
Squid is a staple of Adriatic cuisine and is cooked in many ways. Squid risotto, blackened by the squid's natural juices, is a Croatian national favourite.

5 Dalmatian Ham (Pršut)
This air-dried smoked ham, often served as a starter with Pag cheese, is arguably even better than the Italian equivalent.

6 Lamb (Janjetina)
Flavoursome lamb from animals that have been fed on fresh herbs.

7 Lobster (Jastog)
After selecting your lobster from a tank, feast on this decadent dish, which is usually served in a classic way.

8 Pašticada
Dalmatia's most famous meat dish is this delicious tangy stew of beef in red wine, plums and tomatoes.

9 Istrian Truffles (Tartufi)
From Croatian Istria, both white and black varieties give French and Italian truffles a run for their money.

10 Grilled Fresh Fish
Dalmatia's signature dish is disarmingly straightforward: fresh fish, grilled as simply as possible. Salt and olive oil are the only other essentials.

For a key to restaurant price ranges see p75

🔟 Gifts and Souvenirs

1 Chocolate

Locally made chocolates are an increasingly important part of the confectionery scene. A dash of Adriatic character is provided by the use of local flavourings: mandarins, lemons, figs, carob (*rogač*), lavender and sea salt are among some of the most common additions.

2 Wine

Quality Dalmatian wines include the reds Plavac, Dingač and Postup from the Pelješac Peninsula. Grk and Pošip (white) are grown in Korčula. Vineyards in the Konavle region produce delectable Dubrovačka Malvazija (also white). Outside of Dalmatia, Žlahtina from the island of Krk, Graševina from Slavonia, and Istrian Malvazija – again all white – are also excellent. It's best to buy direct from the vineyard – otherwise, from a *Vinoteka* (wine shop).

3 Croatian Spirits

Dalmatians are fond of grape-, herb- and fruit-based spirits that come under the general name of *rakija* and are drunk as aperitifs or digestifs. *Lozovača* is made from grapes and is rather like Italian grappa. *Travarica* is the same thing but with the flavoursome addition of local herbs. A number of delicious *rakijas* are made from local fruits, such as fig (*smokva*), carob, bilberry

A range of Croatian spirits

(*borovnica*) and walnut (*orahovača*). Nicely packaged bottles make excellent souvenirs.

A selection of lace souvenirs

4 Lace

Available in many guises, including tablecloths, handkerchiefs and clothing, lace can be bought in boutiques throughout Dalmatia. If you are looking for something really authentic, buy intricate hand-woven lace made by Pag islanders, or pick up a piece crafted by nuns in Hvar town using the leaves of agave plants, which grow on the island.

5 Ties

You could be forgiven for thinking the word "cravat" is French, but it is actually derived from the Croatian word *hrvat*, which literally means Croat. During the Thirty Years' War, the French cavalry noticed that Croatians wore their scarves in a distinctive manner – which they termed *à la cravate* ("Croatian-style"). Quality ties can be bought in branches of the Croata (*see p72*) store in Dubrovnik and Split.

6 Jewellery

Dalmatia is particularly well known for its red Adriatic corals and jewellery. The quality and price of goods depend on the vendor. Upmarket boutiques in Hvar town and on the island of Zlarin are reliable for contemporary coral pieces. Jewellers in Zadar and Dubrovnik are good for silver and gold.

7 Lavender

This fragrant plant has been cultivated on Hvar for the past 75 years, and the myriad oils and balms produced provide an important source of revenue for the islanders. In late spring and early summer, the scent of lavender pervades the island, and a host of products are sold at stalls around Hvar town.

8 Food

Paški sir (Pag cheese), *pršut* (air-dried smoked ham), olive oil and honey are all first-rate food products. If you can, buy direct from locals (look out for the handmade signs displayed on the roadside), or from fresh-food markets. Failing that, you will also find these items in supermarkets and tourist shops.

Croatian cured meats

9 Dolls in Traditional Costume

Dolls in traditional dress are ubiquitous throughout Dalmatia. There are dozens of varieties, from cheap and cheerful souvenirs to more expensive figures wearing handmade clothes. Ceramic dolls are a more contemporary version.

10 Local Design

A design boom in Croatia has seen a flurry of local creatives putting their ideas into production. Highly individual bags, brooches, scarves and couture can be picked up in Split and Hvar town. Domestic items are also worth looking out for.

TOP 10 ART AND CRAFTS SHOPS

Delicatessen goods from Uje

1 Uje, Dubrovnik
Quality olive oil is the focus here, but there are also *rakija*, biscuits and soaps *(see p72)*. Branches extend to Bol, Korčula, Split, Trogir and Supetar.

2 Dubrovačka Kuća, Dubrovnik
This is a quality gift shop and art gallery *(see p72)*.

3 Delicium Nostrum, Trogir
MAP B3 ▪ Obrov 2
The perfect place to buy local delicacies and Croatian wines.

4 Sebastian, Dubrovnik
MAP G9 ▪ Svetog Dominika 5
Interesting gallery selling work by famous artists from former Yugoslavia.

5 Prokurative, Split
MAP L2 ▪ Trg Republike
Clothes and accessory designers sell at this open-air weekend market.

6 Sea More, Hvar Town
MAP M3 ▪ Jurja Matijevića 12
Find natural cosmetics made exclusively by Croatian producers.

7 Diocletian's Palace, Split
The souvenir stalls in the main hall stock a wide selection of art *(see p30)*.

8 Bonbonnière Kraš, Dubrovnik
MAP F9 ▪ Obala Stjepana Radića 35
This famous Croatian producer of quality chocolates also sells pralines, biscuits, cookies and liquors.

9 Life According to KAWA, Dubrovnik
MAP H8 ▪ Hvarska 2
This one-stop souvenir and design store is great for cosmetics and wines.

10 Nadalina, Split
MAP N2 ▪ Dioklecijanova 6
Nadalina's unique chocolate bars make highly desirable souvenirs.

🔟 Dubrovnik and the Dalmatian Coast for Free

① Watching Sunsets from the Porporela, Dubrovnik

Dubrovnik is blessed with spectacular Adriatic sunsets, and there are few better places to watch them than the Porporela, the artificial breakwater that stretches eastwards from the Old City. You can reach it by taking the coastal path from the old port.

② Going to the Beach, Dubrovnik

You may have to pay to use a parasol and a sun lounger, but Dubrovnik's beaches are free to all. Just be sure to position your towel on an available space away from the beach bars. Note, however, that you can't reserve a space – towels left out overnight will be confiscated.

③ Coastal Strolls, Dubrovnik

There are any number of seaside promenades on offer outside Dubrovnik's Old City. For a truly scenic walk, take the path that leads from Lapad Beach around the Babin Kuk peninsula, passing coastal rock formations on the way.

④ Scaling Mount Srđ via the Serpentina

Ascending the ridge above Dubrovnik by cable car can be exhilarating, but nothing beats conquering the peak yourself.

Glorious views from the Serpentina

A zigzagging path called the Serpentina will get you there from the Old City in about 80 minutes. The walk is unshaded, so remember to take water and a hat.

⑤ Strolling the Old City Streets of Dubrovnik

In many ways, Dubrovnik's greatest tourist attraction is the Old City itself. Exploring the piazzas and palazzos of this eternally fascinating area will tell you more about the city's history than any museum visit.

⑥ Exploring Diocletian's Palace, Split

It's rare to find a spectacular historical site that can be entered for free, but this is what you get in Diocletian's Palace, which has been adapted over the centuries to form the heart of modern Split. Since it is filled with bars, shops, dwellings and churches, it can't be fenced and an entrance fee charged.

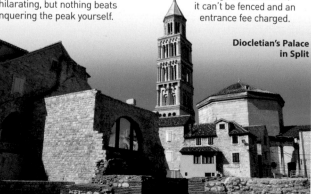
Diocletian's Palace in Split

7 Wandering the Biokovo Botanical Garden

Paths above the resort of Makarska lead up onto the lower slopes of the Biokovo range, the site of a unique botanical garden devoted to highland plants. It is a good introduction to the local flora, and there are also great views of the coast.

8 Relaxing in Đorđić-Mayneri Park, Lopud

Right on the seafront in Lopud, the Đorđić-Mayneri Park is one of the few 19th-century gardens in Dalmatia that has been restored to something approaching its former glory. It is rich in trees, with palm varieties from around the world.

Đorđić-Mayneri Park, Lopud

9 Enjoying the View from Marjan Hill, Split

Marjan, the hilly peninsula that stretches west of central Split, is a huge wooded park that provides the city with its main recreation zone. You can scale the central summit of Telegrin, or walk around the south side to enjoy expansive Adriatic views.

10 Enjoying Street Festivals

Annual feast days and festivals (see pp62–3) fill the streets with revellers until the early morning, giving quiet towns an urban buzz. The big dates are the Feast of St Blaise in Dubrovnik (3 February) and the Feast of St Domnius (7 May) in Split. During the tourist season, events such as the Makarska Cultural Summer (June–August) feature outdoor concerts, with street-party atmospheres.

TOP 10 BUDGET TIPS

Scenic foot-passenger ferry

1 Ferry by Foot
Don't take a car on a ferry to the islands. It's cheaper to travel as a foot passenger and hire a car when you arrive.

2 Stay in an Apartment
A self-catering apartment will usually be cheaper than a hotel room for the same number of people.

3 Visit Independent Cafés
Grab your morning coffee outside Dubrovnik's Old City in a bar used by locals. It will be cheaper (and many say better).

4 Eat at Small Restaurants
Look for restaurants with daily specials or set lunches listed on a board outside.

5 Off-Peak Trips
Accommodation prices are at their height from June to September. Travel out of season for money-saving deals.

6 Buy a Big Parasol
Invest in your own beach parasol or tent in order to avoid the high daily rental costs.

7 Drink Local
Sample the excellent local wines instead of choosing the more expensive imported varieties.

8 Scenic Slow Boats
Take the slow boat to the islands by travelling with ferries rather than the faster but more expensive catamarans.

9 Make Your Own Meals
Skip restaurants altogether by stocking up on delicious local cheeses, hams and fruits at local markets.

10 Buy Return Tickets
If you are travelling along the coast by bus, purchasing a return ticket will be cheaper than buying two singles.

Festivals and Events

① Feast of St Blaise, Dubrovnik

On 3 February, Dubrovnik's citizens mark the life and work of their patron saint and protector *(see p45)*. The celebrations begin at 10am, with a Mass outside the cathedral. At 11:30am, reliquaries of St Blaise are carried around the city.

② Carnival

Spectacular Shrove Tuesday processions are held in Split, where masked locals burn an effigy of Krnje, a mythical figure that represents all the ills that have befallen the city over the previous year. On the same day, in a celebration known as Poklad, the inhabitants of Lastovo commemorate a 15th-century victory of the islanders over pirates; a puppet is chased, captured and burned at the stake.

③ Feast of St Domnius, Split

Split's patron saint is celebrated on 7 May, with locals lining the Riva to watch the religious procession before heading to the Palace area. Stalls on the Riva sell souvenirs of the day.

④ Mediterranean Film Festival, Split

Early Jun ■ www.fmfs.hr

This week-long festival showcases new films with a Southern European focus. Screenings take place at the Zlatna Vrata cinema in the Palace district and at the outdoor cinema on the beach at Bačvice.

⑤ Midsummer Scene Festival, Dubrovnik

Mid-Jun & Jul ■ www.midsummer-scene.com

Lovrijenac Fortress *(see p69)* makes an enchanting venue for this open-air summer festival – the only festival of English theatre in southeast Europe. Named after Shakespeare's *A Midsummer Night's Dream*, this festival has grown in its offerings since its inception in 2014; enjoy comedy and live music, all performed under the stars.

⑥ Split Summer Festival

Mid-Jul–late Aug ■ www.splitsko-ljeto.hr

Opera, ballet, classical music, pop, and a diverse array of theatrical performances heighten the energy -in Dalmatia's largest city. Open-air productions held in Diocletian's Palace *(see pp30–31)* are the highlight, with the staging of Verdi's *Aida* in the Peristyle an enduring favourite.

⑦ Dubrovnik Summer Festival

Mid-Jul–late Aug ■ www.dubrovnik-festival.hr

For several decades, stages in historic venues, churches and the open air

Performers at the Dubrovnik Festival

have filled the Old City with theatre, dance and music. Performances of Shakespeare in the Lovrijenac Fortress tend to sell out quickly.

8 Moreška, Korčula Town

This traditional 15th-century sword-dance (see p26), staged in Korčula town on the Feast of St Theodore (29 July) and on Mondays and Thursdays in high season, portrays White and Black kings fighting for the affections of a beautiful maiden. This war dance is accompanied with music from a brass band.

The Moreška sword-dance

9 Stories of Diocletian, Split

Late Aug

The history, culture and legacy of Emperor Diocletian and his iconic palace in Split are explored through a rich interactive and educational program of events. Expect recreations of key moments from the emperor's life and reign, and learn more about the city through the stories narrated.

10 Summer Festivals

In July and August, summer festivals last from 2 weeks to 2 months, with dance, theatre and music gracing outdoor and indoor stages. Some of the liveliest festivals are held in Cavtat, Hvar town, Makarska, Ston and Trogir.

TOP 10 VENUES

Poljud Stadium, Split

1 Poljud Stadium, Split
Home to Hajduk Split football team, the Poljud also hosts rock concerts and other music events.

2 Rector's Palace, Dubrovnik
Classical concerts are staged in the open-air atrium (see pp18–19) from April to October.

3 Sponza Palace, Dubrovnik
Atmospheric venue in the inner courtyard of this 16th-century palace (see p14).

4 Church of St Saviour, Dubrovnik
This Renaissance church (see p15) in the Old City hosts classical concerts every Monday at 9pm.

5 Town Theatre, Hvar Town
Trg Svetog Stjepana ▪ 021 742 935
One of Europe's earliest theatres.

6 Open-Air Theatre, Korčula Town
This compact circular arena overlooks the harbour and offers stunning views of the Pelješac Peninsula.

7 Orsula Park, Dubrovnik
This unique outdoor venue in a natural amphitheatre overlooks a medieval chapel and the Adriatic coast.

8 Open-Air Cinema, Vis Town
Of all Croatia's summer cinemas, this is the most charming, situated right by the sea on Vis town's beautiful bay.

9 Croatian National Theatre, Split
Trg Gaje Bulata 1 ▪ 021 306 908
Impressive theatre hosting opera, ballet and classical music performances.

10 Marin Držić Theatre, Dubrovnik
Pred Dvorom 3 ▪ 020 321 088
Ornate venue staging a wide-ranging theatrical programme.

Dubrovnik and the Dalmatian Coast Area by Area

Boats moored at the pretty waterfront in Komiža, on the island of Vis

🔟 Dubrovnik

Byron called it "The Pearl of the Adriatic". George Bernard Shaw suggested it was "paradise on earth". Now fully recovered from

Column from the Rector's Palace

the Serbian and Montenegrin siege of 1991–2, this remarkable former city-state has perhaps the most attractive and well-preserved Baroque core of any European city. Its swathe of churches, palaces and old stone houses are contained within the sturdy walls that have protected its famed *libertas* (freedom) for centuries. Much of what you see today is the result of painstaking reconstruction after the 1667 earthquake; now, new building work is strictly controlled, even down to the shade of green to be used on the shutters of the city's main thoroughfare, the Stradun.

1 Cathedral

MAP G10 ■ Poljana Marina Držića ■ 020 323 459 ■ Treasury: open Apr–Jun, Sep & Oct: 9am–5pm Mon–Sat (from 11am Sun); Jul & Aug: 8am–6pm Mon–Sat (from 11am Sun); Nov–Mar: 10am–noon & 3–5pm Mon–Sat, 11am–noon & 3–5pm Sun ■ Adm

Erected after the 1667 earthquake, today's Baroque cathedral *(see p45)*, crafted by Italian architects, replaced

View over Dubrovnik's Old City

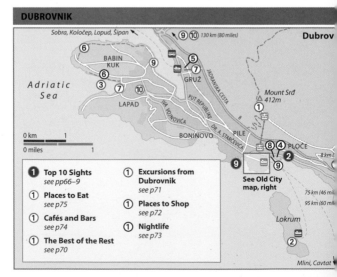

DUBROVNIK

Sobra, Koločep, Lopud, Šipan

Dubrov

130 km (80 miles)

Adriatic Sea

BABIN KUK

GRUŽ

JADRANSKA CESTA

PUT REPUBLIKE

Mount Srđ
△ 412m

LAPAD

VIA VOJNOVIĆA

DR. A. STARČEVIĆA

BONINOVO

PILE

PLOČE

0 km   1
0 miles   1

8 km l

See Old City map, right

75 km (46 mil
95 km (60 mil

Lokrum

Mlini, Cavtat

an earlier Romanesque structure. It houses more than 200 reliquaries, including a 12th-century Byzantine case containing the skull of St Blaise, and casks containing his hands and one leg. It also has what is claimed to be a fragment of the cross on which Jesus was crucified, and a copy of Raphael's *Virgin of the Chair,* reputedly made by the grand master himself.

2 Museum of Modern Art, Dubrovnik

MAP K9 ■ Put Frana Supila 23 ■ 020 426 590 ■ Open 9am–8pm Tue–Sun ■ Adm ■ www.momad.hr

Housed in a Neo-Renaissance-cum-Gothic-style villa in Ploče, this museum has sculptures by Ivan Meštrović (1883–1962) *(see p46)* and portraits by Vlaho Bukovac (1855–1922).

3 Dominican Monastery

MAP G8 ■ Svetog Dominika 4 ■ 020 322 200 ■ Open May–Oct: 9am–6pm daily (Nov–Apr: to 5pm) ■ Adm

The Dominicans were allowed into the city in the 14th century as long as they helped to protect its eastern entrance, where they began building this monastery in 1315. The monastery

The Dominican monastery and port

buildings of today – the church and library – were spared damage by the 1667 earthquake, which only impacted the south wall and the roof, now both restored. Highlights include the Gothic cloisters, 14th-century Italian painter Paolo Veneziano's *Crucifixion* (in the church), and the museum, which houses Titian's *St Blaise, St Mary Magdalene, the Angel Tobias and the Purchaser* – the man on his knees is a member of the then-powerful Gučetić (Gozze) family who funded the work.

4 Rector's Palace

The post of Rector of Dubrovnik was one which each incumbent held for just one month. For that brief period, this was his home *(see pp18–19).*

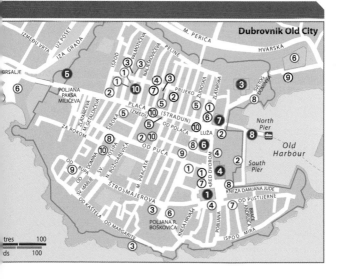

Dubrovnik Old City

5 City Walls

There are few better ways to begin your exploration of Dubrovnik than a walk around the city walls (see pp12–13).

6 Church of St Blaise

The original 14th-century church survived the 1667 earthquake (see p15) largely intact, only to burn down in a fire in 1706. Work started on the present incarnation later the same year, to plans by Italian architect Marino Gropelli, who based the design of the interior on that of a Baroque church in his home town. Punctuating the ornate façade are four pillars watched over by an array of saints (see p45). The stained-glass windows are also striking – a late-20th-century addition of an unusual kind in this part of Europe.

Stone mask on a fountain in the Old City

7 Stradun and Sponza Palace

The main artery of the Old City is the Stradun (see pp14–15), a stone-paved strip that runs past a stately row of houses that was built after the earthquake of 1667. One of the few buildings that survived the quake was Paskoje Miličević's Sponza Palace (1506–22) at the eastern end of the Stradun. Featuring Renaissance arcades and Venetian-Gothic windows, it is now home to the city archives.

8 Old Harbour
MAP H9

Dubrovnik's first harbour stood to the west side of the city, between the Pile Gate and the Lovrijenac Fortress, but it failed to offer sufficient shelter, and in any case soon became too small as the city grew. The Old Harbour, on the east side of the Old City, is a much grander affair, with the Revelin and St John's forts guarding either flank. Amenities are limited here, but there are one or two places to eat and take in the busy summer scenes; there's always a flurry of small fishing boats and tourist craft enjoying the harbour's protection, and there are good views down the coast towards Cavtat.

A sunny panorama across Dubrovnik Old Harbour

The imposing Lovrijenac Fortress

⑨ Lovrijenac Fortress

MAP J9 ▪ 020 638 800
▪ Open Apr & early Sep: 8am–6:30pm
daily (May & Aug: to 7pm; Jun & Jul:
to 7:30pm; mid–late Sep: to 6pm
daily; early Oct: to 5:30pm; mid–late
Oct: to 5pm); Nov–Mar: 9am–3pm
daily ▪ Adm

This fortress rises steeply out of the
Adriatic to the west of the city walls.
Historically, it served both as a place
to store the city's gold and a military
hub and battery where the city could
be brought to heel in the event of a
rebellion. The city's slogan guards
the entrance:"Freedom must not be
sold for all the gold in the world."
The fortress is one of the most
atmospheric venues of the Dubrovnik
Festival (see pp62–3). It's a tough
climb on a hot day, but worth it.

⑩ War Photo Limited

MAP F9 ▪ Antuninska 6 ▪ 020
322 166 ▪ Open May & Oct: 10am–
4pm daily (Jun–Sep: to 9pm)
▪ Closed Nov–Apr ▪ Adm ▪ www.
warphotoltd.com

Just off the Stradun, this exhibition
centre displays works by top war
and conflict photographers. Curated
by New Zealander Wade Goddard,
himself a former war photographer,
the centre exposes the horrors and
ugliness of war. Its exhibitions are
thought-provoking, informative
and often heartbreaking. The
centre shows the photographs as
traditional framed prints or as
digital presentations. One room
holds a permanent display of
images and multimedia from the
conflicts that tore Yugoslavia apart
in the 1990s.

A DAY IN DUBROVNIK

▶ MORNING

If you're an early riser, climb the
City Walls when they open (9am)
and you may have them largely
to yourself. Make a leisurely circuit
taking in their sights (see pp12–13)
and watching the city as it grad-
ually comes to life below. Stop
at **St John's Fort** (see p13)
to learn about Dubrovnik's sea-
faring history at the **Maritime
Museum** (see p46). Descend to
the Stradun (see pp14–15), and if
you didn't take breakfast at your
hotel, enjoy a coffee and a pastry
at the **Festival Café** (see p74) –
it's a great vantage-point from
which to observe the frenetic
street life of the city's main artery.

Continue strolling gently down
the Stradun, absorbing the
atmosphere rather than delving
into its various attractions. Enjoy
an early seafood lunch at noon in
Kamenice (see p75), then absorb
the colourful sights and sounds
of the market in **Gundulićeva
Poljana** (see p70).

AFTERNOON

After lunch, head across to the
Rector's Palace (see pp18–19)
and take a self-guided audio tour.
Continue around to the start of
the Stradun at Luža Square. From
here you can choose which of this
pedestrianized area's attractions
to explore (see pp14–15) as you
travel its length towards the **Pile
Gate** (see p12). Here, enjoy a warm
welcome at the **Café Dubravka**
(see p74) or perhaps take an early
dinner at **Nautika** (see p75), which
grants glorious views over one of
Europe's most stunning cities.

See map on pp66–7 ⬅

The Best of the Rest

Statue in Gundulićeva Poljana

1 Gundulićeva Poljana (Gundulić Square)
MAP G9

This beautiful square is home to a statue of Ivan Gundulić, the 17th-century poet whose *Osman* recalls a great Slavic victory over the Turks. There's a lively morning market here.

2 Orthodox Church Museum
MAP F9 ▪ Od Puča 8 ▪ 020 323 283
▪ Closed for renovation, call ahead
▪ Adm

Two doors down from the Serbian Orthodox Church *(see p45)* is this colourful Icon Museum, which has ecclesiastical art dating from the 15th to 19th centuries. There are modern portraits on display too.

3 Church of St Ignatius
MAP F10 ▪ Poljana R Boškovića
▪ Open 8am–7pm daily

Up a grand sweep of stairs, modelled on Rome's Spanish Steps, is this 18th-century Jesuit Church that houses fine examples of trompe l'oeil.

4 Pustijerna
MAP G10

Wander the streets of this area to the south of the Stradun in search of traces of the city walls. Medieval houses, many in ruins, huddle along impossibly narrow lanes, giving an insight into pre-1667 Dubrovnik.

5 Synagogue
MAP G9 ▪ Žudioska 5 ▪ Open Apr–Oct: 10am–8pm daily; Nov–Mar: 9am–3pm daily ▪ Adm

The Synagogue is said to be Europe's second oldest, after the one in Prague.

6 Archaeology Collection
MAP H8 ▪ Revelin Fort
▪ 020 324 041 ▪ Open Apr–Oct: 9am–6pm Thu–Tue (Nov–Mar: to 4pm)
▪ Adm

This small exhibition is on the lower storeys of the 16th-century Revelin Fort. Many of the stone carvings once adorned the city's churches.

7 Red History Museum
MAP J8 ▪ Svetog Križa 3
▪ 020 205 247 ▪ Open Apr–Oct: 10am–8pm daily; Nov–Mar: 11am–5pm Tue–Sat ▪ Adm

Experience life during the Yugoslavian regime through interactive exhibits here. Step into a reconstructed flat dating from Tito's time, or delve into art and design styles of that period.

8 Dulčić-Masle-Pulitika Gallery
MAP G10 ▪ Držićeva poljana 1
▪ 020 612 645 ▪ Open 9am–8pm Tue–Sun ▪ Adm

Works by Ivo Dulčić (1916–75), Antun Masle (1919–67) and Đuro Pulitika (1922–2006) are on display here.

9 Rupe Ethnographic Museum
MAP F9 ▪ Od Rupa 3 ▪ 020 323 013
▪ Open Apr–Oct: 9am–6pm Wed–Mon (Nov–Mar: to 4pm Thu–Tue)
▪ Adm

Built to store grain in case of a siege, this museum represents the cultural heritage and traditions of the inhabitants of the surrounding area.

10 House of Marin Držić
MAP F9 ▪ Široka 7 ▪ Open 9am–8:30pm Tue–Sun ▪ Adm

This museum honours a celebrated 16th-century Dubrovnik playwright.

See map on pp66–7

Excursions from Dubrovnik

1 Mount Srđ
MAP K8

Modern cable cars ascend Mount Srđ in fewer than four minutes for amazing views. The Napoleonic fortress at the summit holds a museum devoted to the 1991–2 siege.

2 Lokrum

Temptingly positioned just offshore is an unspoiled island *(see pp20–21)* that is a world away from the city, with quiet coves, an old monastery and a crumbling fort. Boats leave from the old port.

3 Lapad Bay
MAP H8

Squeezed between the Lapad and Babin Kuk peninsulas, this broad shallow bay is home to one of Dubrovnik's most popular family beaches. The pedestrianized Kralja Zvonimira is abuzz with cafés.

4 Srebreno
MAP H6

Right next to Mlini, Srebreno is an up-and-coming resort, with a plush hotel and shopping mall overlooking its broad sweep of a bay. The shoreline promenade takes you past busy cafés and a children's playpark.

5 Mlini
MAP H6

This small fishing village 11 km (7 miles) south of Dubrovnik has a palm-lined waterfront and traditional stone houses. Numerous streams and a beach add to Mlini's appeal.

6 Babin Kuk Peninsula
MAP J8

Sharing the same rump of land as Lapad, Babin Kuk is another beach-lined peninsula that is a pleasant area for walking and swimming.

7 Kotor
MAP K7

Cross the border into Montenegro, and your reward is the nearest the Adriatic has to a fjord – the stunning Kotor Bay – and the charming historical town of Kotor itself.

8 Sveti Stefan

Further on into Montenegro, this hotel resort on its own island was once a favourite of the international jet set. Today's day-trippers can walk the island and dine in the restaurant.

9 Mostar

The old bridge that gave the city its name has been expertly restored following its notorious destruction during the 1990s conflict. It is the top sight in this city *(see p91)* in Bosnia-Herzegovina, close to the Croatian border.

10 Međugorje
MAP F4

Even during the war, pilgrims flocked to this spot in Bosnia-Herzegovina, where the Virgin Mary is said to have appeared in 1981. Hordes of visitors have tainted things a bit, but this is still a remarkable place to visit.

Boats in the bay at Mlini

Places to Shop

① Modni Kantun
MAP G9 ■ Zlatarska 3

Tucked into an alley behind the Sponza Palace, "Fashion Corner" specializes in clothes by Croatian designers and features many practical, stylish and unique designs. They also stock hats, bags and jewellery.

② Dubrovačka Kuća (Dubrovnik House)
MAP H9 ■ Svetog Dominika bb

This is a charming gallery-meets-gift shop selling quality Croatian wines, Istrian truffles, traditional souvenirs and original paintings.

③ Enoteca Wine Shop
MAP G9 ■ Prijeko 28

A great wine shop near the Stradun, Enoteca sells an impressive selection of Croatian wines. Tastings are also on offer here.

④ Medusa
MAP G8 ■ Prijeko 18

Great for souvenir shopping, Medusa stocks Croatian products such as original, handmade Croatian craftwork, wooden toys, natural cosmetics and local food. It also exhibits paintings by local artists.

The entrance to Medusa

⑤ Algebra
MAP G9 ■ Placa 9

This centrally located bookstore is a great place to browse through a wide range of books, including works by Croatian writers translated into English. It is also a useful shop for visitors wanting to pick up travel guides and souvenirs.

⑥ Tilda
MAP G9 ■ Zlatarska 1

A tiny souvenir shop tucked between the Stradun and Prijeko, Tilda stocks a range of traditional clothes and handmade accessories, including bags with intricate hand-embroidery.

⑦ Croata
MAP G9 ■ Pred Dvorom 2

Where better to buy a tie than the country in which they were created? At Croata visitors can shop for ties, scarves and shawls, handmade from the finest silk, with unique designs. There are also branches in Split.

⑧ Terra Croatica
MAP F9 ■ Ulica od puča 17

Head to this gift shop, which specializes in sweet and savoury local delicacies. Expect olive oils, honey, jams, chocolate, wines, brandies and liqueurs, as well as locally designed arts and crafts.

⑨ Life According to KAWA
MAP H8 ■ Hvarska 2

Located above Ploče Gate, this delightful store sells local delicacies, craft beer, wine and award-winning olive oil, as well as clothes and ceramics designed by local designers and artisans.

⑩ Uje
MAP G9 ■ Placa bb

Uje is one of the main outlets for quality Croatian olive oil, notably their own-brand Brachia, a smooth aromatic oil from the island of Brač. It also sells a range of preserves, local capers and chocolates.

Nightlife

1 Nonenina
MAP G9 ■ Pred Dvorom 4

This centrally located bar has outdoor tables and comfy seating looking out onto the Rector's Palace, making it a perfect spot for evening cocktails.

2 Casablanca Bar
MAP G9 ■ Zamanjina 7

Located in the heart of the Old Town, this bar shares many similarities with Rick's café in the 1942 film *Casablanca*. It has been one of Dubrovnik's best-loved bars for decades, with young locals and visitors alike flocking here to drink and dance the night away.

3 Buzz Bar
MAP G9 ■ Prijeko 21

Located on a parallel street to the Stradun, Buzz Bar is a favourite with locals and visitors for its lively atmosphere. A classic cocktail menu, along with a good stock of craft beer and local wine, help ensure the bar's enduring popularity.

4 Banje Beach Club
MAP H8 ■ Frana Supila 10b

This chic club on Banje Beach is the place to party come sunset, with magical views of the floodlit city walls across the water.

5 Dubina Club
MAP F8 ■ Ulica Svetog Križa 3

Housed in an old factory near Gruž harbour, Dubina has been popular since opening in 2022. It provides a platform for local DJs and bands who play a range of music, including jazz, house, funk and techno.

6 Cave Bar More
MAP J8 ■ Nika i Meda Pucića 13

Situated in a natural cave, this bar has outdoor tables overlooking Lapad Bay. It is a beautiful spot to have great cocktails or just a glass of local beer while enjoying the sunset.

7 The Bar by Azur
MAP G8 ■ Kunićeva 5

Popular with locals, this fine bar spread over two levels offers excellent cocktails. There's also a good range of craft brews, gins and Croatian wines.

Contemporary venue Club Lazareti

8 Club Lazareti
MAP H8 ■ Frana Supila 8

An old quarantine house and artisans' workshops now form a venue for alternative, contemporary musical, and theatrical performances and a nightclub with guest DJs. There is an outdoor terrace and direct access to Komarda beach too, where parties are often held in the summer. Check their social media to see what's on.

9 Culture Club Revelin
MAP H9 ■ Svetog Dominika 3

Every night the Revelin fort becomes the centre of Dubrovnik's nightlife scene, hosting the world's best DJs and chart-topping performers.

10 Cele Dubrovnik Gourmet & Lounge
MAP G9 ■ Placa 1

A sedate café-bar by day, Cele transforms into a lively nighttime spot once the sun goes down. It also hosts live music performances.

See map on pp66–7 ←

Cafés and Bars

Cosy interior of D'Vino Wine Bar

1 D'Vino Wine Bar
MAP F9 ■ Palmotićeva 4a

This friendly little wine bar, in the heart of the Old City, serves quality Dalmatian wine by the glass or bottle. It is a cosy place with exposed stone walls and subtle lighting.

2 Festival Café
MAP F9 ■ Placa bb

At the western end of the Stradun, this café has a mellow and sophisticated air. Director's chairs on the pavement are great for watching the world go by. If you've been hankering after single-malt Scotch whisky, look no further.

3 Buža
MAP F10 ■ off Od Margarite

On a sunny day, follow the signs from Gundulićeva Poljana (see p70) to this great open-air bar. Located on the rocks outside the southern walls of the Old City, it has great views over the sea to Lokrum.

4 Gradska Kavana
MAP G9 ■ Pred Dvorom 1

This revamped city café has a terrace that is in the perfect place for a spot of people watching.

5 Le Petit Belge Pub
MAP F8 ■ Vetranićeva 3

Tucked away in a quiet side alley off the Stradun, this pub has a huge selection of Belgian beers, with Croatian craft options available too. Unwind with a drink in the outdoor seating area.

6 Café Dubravka 1836
MAP E8 ■ Brsalje 3

The views from this low-key café's terrace are spectacular. It is located between the Pile Gate and the Lovrijenac Fortress.

7 Lapad Beach
MAP J8 ■ Lapad Bay

This complex on the beach at Lapad Bay combines a restaurant, bar and lounge terrace. It's great for drinks and snacks by day, and, once the sun goes down, a party vibe takes over.

8 La Bodega
MAP G9 ■ Lučarica 1

At the eastern end of the Stradun is La Bodega, which occupies the ground floor and three storeys of a historic house. A different experience is offered on each, from café to wine and tapas bar to party space.

9 Café & Restaurant Lucijan
MAP G9 ■ Gundulićeva poljana bb

Soak up the atmosphere of Gundulić square while sipping Croatian wine at this café. On sunny days, nab a Parisian-style street table outside, or take a seat in the cosy interior.

10 The Gaffe Pub
MAP G9 ■ Miha Pracata 4

The Gaffe Pub is a more refined version of the Irish theme bar across the street, with a green and dark-wood decor. The staff are friendly, and the atmosphere is relaxed.

The Irish-themed Gaffe Pub

Places to Eat

① Nishta
MAP F8 ▪ Prijeko bb ▪ 020 322 088 ▪ €€

Dubrovnik's first vegan restaurant has a superb salad bar and offers Indian curries and raw cakes (made with nuts and seeds). Book ahead in summer.

② Lokanda Peskarija
MAP H10 ▪ Na Ponti bb ▪ 020 324 750 ▪ Closed Dec–Feb ▪ €

Lokanda Peskarija serves a simple menu of mussels, squid, shrimp and seafood risotto. Outdoor benches overlook the Old Harbour, and the rustic interior is atmospheric.

③ Kamenice
MAP G10 ▪ Gundulićeva Poljana 8 ▪ 020 323 682 ▪ €

Gorge on huge plates of fried squid, fresh mussels, seafood risotto and grilled scampi, washed down with a crisp house white. It's great value, and the outdoor setting is wonderful.

④ Nautika
MAP E9 ▪ Brsalje 3 ▪ 020 442 526 ▪ Closed Dec–Jan ▪ €€€

Share an Adriatic fish platter or Chateaubriand with a loved one as the Adriatic laps at the rocks below (see pp56–7).

⑤ Fish Restaurant Proto
MAP F9 ▪ Široka 1 ▪ 020 323 234 ▪ €€€

Proto is one of the best restaurants in the Old City, with a menu that focuses on seafood but also caters to meat-eaters. The terrace on the first floor is the place to be in summer.

⑥ Kopun
MAP G10 ▪ Boškovićeva poljana 7 ▪ 020 323 969 ▪ Closed Dec & Jan ▪ €

The charmingly situated Kopun is one of the best places for traditional specialities, such as the roast capon that gives this restaurant its name.

Oyster & Sushi Bar Bota

⑦ Oyster & Sushi Bar Bota
MAP G10 ▪ Od pustijerne bb ▪ 020 324 034 ▪ €€

This chic, romantic spot serves some of the best Croatian-Asian fusion food in the Adriatic – think oysters, sushi and tempura.

⑧ 360
MAP H9 ▪ Sv Dominika bb ▪ 020 322 222 ▪ Closed Mon & Nov–Mar ▪ €€€

A Mediterranean fine-dining menu and huge international wine list are offered in an elegant setting with stunning views of the port.

⑨ Orsan
MAP J8 ▪ Ivana Zajca 2 ▪ 020 436 822 ▪ Closed Dec ▪ €€

Serving classic Dalmatian dishes in a seaside setting, Orsan is popular with locals and tourists alike.

⑩ Pantarul
MAP G6 ▪ Kralja Tomislava 1 ▪ 020 333 486 ▪ Closed Mon ▪ €

This restaurant lives by its motto "feels like home", so expect a casual atmosphere and tasty seasonal dishes.

See map on pp66–7 ←

TOP 10 The Dalmatian Islands

Many of Dalmatia's most spectacular features are at their most concentrated on the islands. Centuries of culture are found in historic towns that blend modern tourist facilities with an intimate, welcoming feel. Island landscapes tend towards the raw and uncommercialized, with olive groves, vineyards and Mediterranean maquis spilling over the dry-stone walls built centuries ago by rock-clearing farmers. The main islands are already established destinations: chic but charming Hvar, beachcomber-friendly Brač, vine-carpeted Korčula and distant, unspoiled Vis – many Croats' favourite Adriatic island. Beach connoisseurs will be delighted by the sheer variety of broad shingle bays and semi-secret coves on offer, and by the remarkably clear sea. While ferries and catamarans from Split provide the main means of transportation, a seaplane service also links some of the main resorts.

Sculpture from Korčula's Cathedral of St Mark

THE DALMATIAN ISLANDS

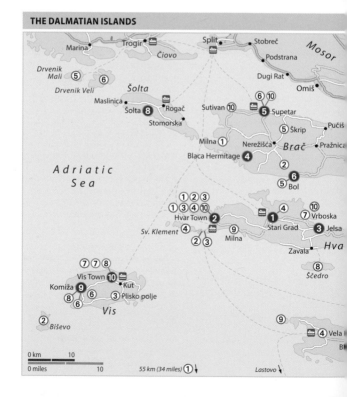

Wooden boats in the harbour at Stari Grad

1 Stari Grad, Hvar
MAP C4 ■ Tourist info: Obala dr. Franje Tuđmana 1; 021 765 763

Founded by the ancient Greeks, Stari Grad was for a long time Hvar's main town. It still serves as the island's main ferry port, but the bustle of traffic is kept well away from the charming centre of medieval streets, window boxes and pretty squares. The harbour, with its ring of stone houses and yachting marina, makes for a delightful stroll. Immediately east of town is the Stari Grad Plain, a UNESCO-protected patchwork of fields that has changed little since ancient Greek times.

2 Hvar Town
MAP C4 ■ Tourist info: Trg sv Stjepana 42; 021 741 059; www.visithvar.hr

Grouped around a horseshoe-shaped harbour, Hvar town is at once a historical town and contemporary tourist playground. The Riva, with its cocktail bars and swanky yachts, is a few steps away from one of the Adriatic's finest squares, where a cathedral, Venetian arsenal and Baroque theatre make for a stunning ensemble. On either side of the square are former aristocratic houses that are now restaurants and specialist shops. There are rocky bathing spots around the town itself, and gorgeous shingle beaches on the Pakleni islands, which is a short water taxi ride across the bay.

3 Jelsa, Hvar
MAP C4 ■ Tourist info: Trg Tome Gamulina 1; 021 761 017; www.tzjelsa.hr

Jelsa is a relatively unspoiled fishing port with good beaches. It can be busy in summer but rarely overpowering. There is a warren of narrow streets at its heart and a seaside path to the village of Vrboska (see p80), 5 km (3 miles) away. Boats leave for Bol every morning.

MARCO POLO

The island of Korčula is alleged to be the birthplace of the explorer Marco Polo – a claim that has been hotly disputed by both Venice and Genoa. Historians now generally agree that Polo was born in the Venetian Republic, but there is evidence that he was imprisoned by the Genoese in Korčula Town, which may be where the legend started. Learn more about him at the Marco Polo Centre (p26).

4 Blaca Hermitage, Brač
MAP C4 ■ 091 516 4671 ■ Open 9am–5pm Tue–Sun (mid-Sep–mid-Jun: to 3pm) ■ Adm

Dramatically situated on the scrub-covered flanks of a ravine, Blaca Hermitage is one of the most-visited former monasteries in Croatia. It was founded in the 16th century by an association of island priests who wanted to establish a monastic community with its own rules. The hermitage can be reached on foot from a car-park a few minutes' uphill walk away.

5 Supetar, Brač
MAP C3 ■ Tourist info: Porat 1, 021 630 551; www.supetar.hr

An hour away from Split by regular ferry, Supetar is the easiest of the island resorts to reach. It's a charming little spot, grouped around a small-boat harbour and overlooked by a pretty parish church. Supetar's main asset is the broad pebbly bay just

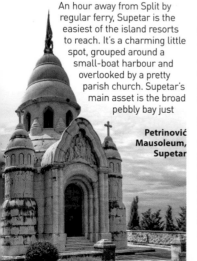

Petrinović Mausoleum, Supetar

west of the harbour – perfect for a lazy day. Behind the beach looms the spire of the Petrinović Mausoleum, a famously elegant funerary chapel designed by Split-born sculptor Toma Rosandić.

Aerial view of Zlatni Rat, Bol

6 Bol, Brač
MAP C4 ■ Tourist info: Porat bolskih pomoraca bb; 021 635 638; www.bol.hr

Spreading beneath the vineyard-covered slopes of Vidova Gora, Bol is one of the most popular resorts in Dalmatia on account of its proximity to Zlatni Rat, the magnificent curve of shingle that juts into the sea just west of town. Home to a constant holiday buzz during the summer season, Bol nonetheless has a tranquil Old Town made up of stone houses and narrow streets. Thanks to favourable winds in the channel dividing Brač from Hvar, Bol is also a major centre for windsurfing and kite-surfing, with a string of agencies on the path towards Zlatni Rat renting gear and offering lessons.

7 Korčula Town
The historic core of Korčula town (see pp26–7) is one of Dalmatia's most dramatic set-pieces. For the visitor, it offers attractive architecture, fine restaurants and tranquil water-side cafés from which to admire dazzling sunsets. The town is also something of an activity centre, with windsurfing, yachting and diving all popular watersports.

8 Šolta Island

MAP B3 ■ Tourist info: 021 554 657; www.visitsolta.com

Close to Split but not very touristy, Šolta is the perfect getaway. Covered in maquis, olive trees and dry-stone walls, the island is the ideal place for hiking or cycling. At the western tip of the island, the port of Maslinica has a small pebble beach and a sea-side walk to Šešula Bay, which is often filled with visiting yachts. The south coast offers beaches and coves, mostly accessible on foot or by boat.

9 Komiža, Vis

MAP B5 ■ Tourist info: Riva sv. Mikule 2; 021 713 455; www.tz-komiza.hr

Dramatically situated Komiža spreads around a compact bay surrounded by green slopes. It is known for its fishing port history. The harbour is backed by narrow alleys, with shingle beaches a short stroll away. The town has two unique churches in the shape of Our Lady of the Pirates (see p44) and the Mušter (see p45).

The pretty town of Komiža

10 Vis Town, Vis

MAP B5 ■ Tourist info: Šetalište Stare Isse 5; 021 717 017; www.tz-vis.hr

Vis is packed with history: here you'll find Roman baths, a medieval monastery, Austrian-era fortifications and lots of evocative Mediterranean alleys. Highlights include the sub-urb of Kut, famous for its elegant Renaissance houses, a museum that's bursting with ancient amphorae, and the British-built King George III Fortress 2 km (1 mile) out of town.

A DAY ON BRAČ ISLAND

▶ MORNING

Catch the ferry from Split to **Supetar**, and enjoy the journey from the open upper deck. Take morning coffee on Supetar's delightful harbour before hiring a car or bike from one of the agencies opposite the ferry dock. Ascend south onto the island's central plateau, where a landscape of olive groves, dry-stone enclosures and wild figs provides plenty of photo opportunities. Take a detour to the village of **Škrip** (see p80), site of the absorbing Island of Brač Museum (see p46). Continue south to the resort of **Bol**, taking an early lunch in one of the many good restaurants along the animated Riva.

AFTERNOON

Walk or take the tourist train to the famous beach of **Zlatni Rat** (see p48), west of Bol. Spend the afternoon swimming, kayaking or wake-boarding. If you have kids, let them loose at the aquapark. When the heat begins to recede in late afternoon, drive to the summit of **Vidova Gora** (see p80) for glorious views across the Adriatic sea before detouring west to explore the arid and desolate landscape surrounding the **Blaca Hermitage**.

Return to Supetar to drop the car off before taking a seaside stroll to the Petrinović Mausoleum. Enjoy an evening drink at Benny's Bar (see p82), or tuck in to a seafood dinner in Supetar's Bistro Palute (see p83), before catching the last ferry back to Split at 10:45pm.

See map on pp76–7

The Best of the Rest

1 Milna, Brač
MAP C4 ■ Tourist office: Riva 5;
021 636 233

On the western side of Brač, Milna is a typical Mediterranean fishing village. Now a popular stop-off for yachtspeople, it has a lively marina and some welcoming restaurants.

2 Vidova Gora, Brač
MAP C4

Soaring dramatically above Bol, the grey escarpment of Vidova Gora is, at 778 m (2,552 ft) above sea level, the highest point on any Dalmatian island. It is accessible by car, bike or a breathtaking 3-hour hike.

3 Plisko Polje, Vis
MAP B5

Most of Vis is rock and scrub, but a green and fertile plain spreads along the southern part of the island, where the village of Plisko Polje is surrounded by vineyards. It's also the site of Dalmatia's only cricket pitch.

4 Vela Luka, Korčula
MAP C5

Korčula town may be the star sight on the island, but don't miss the palm-fringed port of Vela Luka, where Vela Spila cave attests to the presence of prehistoric cultures.

5 Škrip, Brač
MAP C3

Škrip is a well-preserved inland village surrounded by sheep pasture and olive groves. The Island of Brač Museum (see p46) has enthralling displays.

6 Mount Hum, Vis
MAP B5

One of the Adriatic's great lookout points, the 587-m (1,926-ft) Mount Hum looms above Komiža on the western side of Vis, offering an expansive panorama.

7 Vrboska, Hvar
MAP C4 ■ Tourist office:
Vrboska 404; 021 774 137

The pretty village of Vrboska is famed for its location on either side of a saltwater channel. The nearby Glavica peninsula is a long rocky beach with naturist-friendly coves.

8 Sućuraj, Hvar
MAP E4 ■ Tourist office: Riva bb; 021 717 288

Sućuraj's quiet harbour offers a total contrast to the western Hvar. It's a good choice for beachcombers, with a long stretch of shingle near the centre, and many rocky bays at hand.

9 Milna, Hvar
MAP C4

Just 5 km (3 miles) out of Hvar town, Milna is a largely modern village set in a narrow fold of the island's steep south-facing coast. The Mala Milna shingle beach is a short walk away.

10 Sutivan, Brač
MAP C3 ■ Tourist office: Trg dr. Franje Tuđmana 1; 021 638 357

The fishing port of Sutivan, just west of Supetar, has long stretches of pebbly beach. It's one of Dalmatia's most bicycle-friendly spots, with many marked trails.

Street view of Škrip village, Brač

Smaller Islands

Palagruža with its lighthouse

1 Palagruža (nr Vis)

This rocky slip of land extends out into the Adriatic to the very edge of Croatian waters. The 100-m- (330-ft-) tall lighthouse is the sole structure on the island, which can be reached by private boat.

2 Biševo (nr Vis)

This stunning necklace of unspoiled islands is a paradise for sailors and day-trippers *(see pp22–3)*. For the ultimate escape, head to a deserted island for a taste of "Robinson Crusoe tourism".

3 Jerolim (nr Hvar)
MAP C4

The nearest of the Pakleni islands to Hvar town, Jerolim is celebrated for its many beautiful beaches. This small island is easily explored on foot.

4 Sveti Klement (nr Hvar)
MAP B4

The largest and most varied of the Pakleni islands, Sveti Klement offers a laid-back resort at Palmižana, complete with a beach, restaurants and cactus-filled gardens. Trails lead to quieter areas, with rocky beaches and the occasional rustic restaurant.

5 Drvenik Mali (nr Trogir)
MAP A3

Not actually within the Kornati National Park (as some tour operators say), Drvenik Mali is still a lovely place to spend the day, or to anchor a yacht for an afternoon.

6 Drvenik Veli (nr Trogir)
MAP B3

Connected by a bridge to Ugljan, this island is home to a couple of modest fishing villages and a Benedictine monastery. There are ferry connections to Biograd na Moru.

7 Badija (nr Korčula)
MAP E5

Just off Korčula – and reached by a water taxi – this small island is home to a community of Franciscan monks. The Franciscan church and monastery are both well preserved and make a striking sight by the sea.

The church and monastery on Badija

8 Šćedro (between Hvar and Korčula)
MAP C5

A safe harbour for sea travellers since ancient times, this small island is now a protected nature park.

9 Proizd (nr Korčula)

A short boat ride from Vela Luka, Proizd *(see p49)* is famous for a trio of beaches that consist of shelving slabs of rock. The island is at its most beautiful at sunset when the rocks turn orange and pink.

10 Zečevo (nr Vrboska, Hvar)
MAP C4

Popular with yachtspeople and day-trippers, Zečevo ("Bunny Island") gets its name from the wild rabbits living in its dense shrubbery. Pristine seas and rock beaches attract predominantly naturist bathers.

See map on pp76–7

Cafés, Bars and Nightlife

The Hula beach bar, Hvar town

1 Hula Hula, Hvar Town
MAP C4

This wooden, beachside bar on the coastal path, 15 minutes' walk west of the town, is much loved for its delicious cocktails, ambient music and amazing sunset views.

2 Carpe Diem Beach, Pakleni Islands
MAP C4 ▪ Stipanska uvala

Five minutes by boat from Hvar town, this luxurious restaurant turns into a party venue by night, with an impressive DJ line-up.

3 Sweet Republic, Hvar Town
MAP C4 ▪ Kroz Grodu 20

This café serves homemade raw and vegan cakes, plus pralines, organic coffee, and fresh juices and smoothies made from locally grown, seasonal ingredients.

4 Carpe Diem Bar, Hvar Town
MAP C4 ▪ Riva 3

A fixture of Hvar's harbour since 1998, Carpe Diem Bar is the perfect place to start your day with a coffee on the seafront terrace, overlooked by palm trees. It's equally perfect for a sundowner, when the bar's expert mixologists craft innovative cocktails to the sounds of lounge music.

5 Varadero, Bol
MAP C4 ▪ Frane Radića 1

In the centre of Bol, on the island of Brač, is this immensely popular summer bar overlooking the harbour. Cocktails are served to clientele lounging on comfy wicker sofas under straw umbrellas. There are live DJ sets most nights.

6 Benny's Bar, Supetar
MAP C3 ▪ Put Vele Luke bb

At one end of Supetar's beach, Benny's is at the heart of pretty much everything in town, serving the beach bar crowd during the day, and offering cocktails and DJs at night.

7 Frutarija, Vis Town
MAP B5 ▪ Viški boj 13

Overlooking the sea, this little open-air bar offers stunning views. It serves delicious breakfast, brunch and snacks, as well as juices and cocktails.

8 Fabrika, Komiža, Vis
MAP B5 ▪ Riva svetog Mikule 12

Fabrika combines a lazy lounge-bar vibe with the buzz of a local pub, serving local wines, *rakijas* (fruit spirits) and a small menu of burgers and light meals.

9 Massimo, Korčula Town
MAP E5 ▪ Šetalište Petra Kanavelića bb

Atop one of the town's defensive bastions, this popular summer bar has a unique pulley system for drinks. Appreciate the sunset as the swallows swirl on the skyline.

10 Red Baron, Hvar Town
MAP C4 ▪ Riva bb

This is the perfect location on Hvar town's Riva, ideal for watching the catamaran dock or luxury yachts nearby. With a good choice of shooters, cocktails and spirits, this is one of the island's better-stocked bars.

Places to Eat

PRICE CATEGORIES

For a three-course meal for one with half a bottle of wine (or equivalent meal), taxes and extra charges.

€ up to €50   €€ €50–75
€€€ over €75

1 Macondo, Hvar Town
MAP C4 ▪ Marije Maričić 7 ▪ 021 742 850 ▪ Closed Nov–Apr ▪ €€

This fairly pricey, top-quality seafood restaurant in Hvar's Old Town is no longer a local secret, so book ahead. In summer you can eat outside.

2 Gariful, Hvar Town
MAP M6 ▪ Riva 21 ▪ 021 742 999 ▪ Closed Nov–Mar ▪ €€€

The place to see and be seen in Hvar, this luxurious restaurant serves high-end Mediterranean cuisine. Enjoy lobster on the terrace, where fine views await.

Chic interior of Giaxa, Hvar town

3 Giaxa, Hvar Town
MAP C4 ▪ Petra Hektorovića 11 ▪ 021 741 073 ▪ €€

Fine dining in a former Renaissance palace, with local fish and seafood given a modern European treatment. The desserts are outstanding and the wine list as good as any in town.

4 Antika, Stari Grad
MAP C4 ▪ Donja kola ▪ 099 798 1734 ▪ €€

Just inland from Stari Grad's seafront, Antika serves traditional seafood in a dining room full of knick-knacks and curios. There's an outdoor terrace in the flowery piazza around the corner.

5 Adio Mare, Korčula Town
MAP E5 ▪ Marka Pola 2 ▪ 020 711 253 ▪ Closed Nov–Mar ▪ €€

Located in the Old Town, Adio Mare (see p57) is a lively place to eat on a summer night. Grilled fish is the highlight.

6 Jastožera, Komiža
MAP B5 ▪ Gundulićeva 6 ▪ 091 984 2513 ▪ €€€

Locally caught lobster is the speciality at this restaurant, but it offers a lot more like fresh fish, grilled or baked.

7 Vila Kaliopa, Vis Town
MAP B5 ▪ Vladimira Nazora 32 ▪ 091 271 1755 ▪ Closed Oct–Apr ▪ €€€

Top-notch seafood is served in a sculpture-laden garden of Vila Kaliopa.

8 Pojoda, Vis Town
MAP B5 ▪ Don Cvjetka Marasovića 8 ▪ 021 711 575 ▪ €€

This upmarket restaurant, with an ornate courtyard, charges by the kilo for quality fish. The fine food comes with a wine list and service to match.

9 Konoba Marco Polo, Korčula Town
MAP E5 ▪ Jakova Baničevića 9 ▪ 020 715 643 ▪ Closed mid-Oct–mid-Apr ▪ €€

Tucked away in a side alley in Korčula's Old Town, Konoba Marco Polo is well-regarded for its fish dishes, such as tuna steak, served with quality wines. It's an intimate spot with indoor and outdoor seating.

10 Bistro Palute, Supetar, Brač
MAP C3 ▪ Porat 4 ▪ 021 631 730 ▪ €

Palute offers a large menu of local seafood but has plenty of soups, stews and pasta dishes besides. In summer, tables are placed on a small pier right on Supetar harbour.

See map on pp76–7 ←

TOP 10 The Makarska Riviera and Split

The Makarska Riviera is one of the most picturesque parts of the Dalmatian Coast. Sheltered by the rocky backdrop of the Biokovo mountain range, this long stretch of coast is filled with sandy beaches, lush vegetation, and historic towns and cities. Traces of the various civilizations that have swept through the region emerge colourfully, with Roman remnants at the ruined town of Salona, Ottoman strongholds such as the imposing fortress at Klis, and monuments to Venetian rule in Trogir's historic centre. Split, built around the remnants of Diocletian's Palace, is a vibrant and modern metropolis. As Croatia's second biggest city, it is also a busy transport hub, with regular ferries to the nearby islands. This stunning corner of Croatia seems on an inexorable rise.

Clock tower in Diocletian's Palace, Split

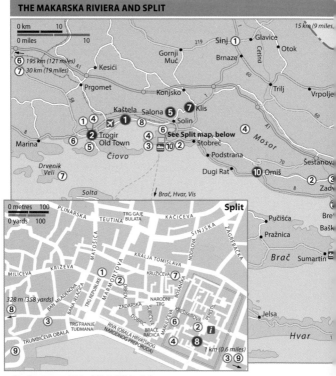

THE MAKARSKA RIVIERA AND SPLIT

Previous pages Waterfalls in Plitvice Lakes

1 Kaštela

MAP B3 ■ Tourist info: Kamberovo šetalište 30, Vila Nika, Kaštel Stari; 021 227 933; www. kastela-info.hr

Nestled between Split and Trogir, the hidden gems of Kaštela await discovery. The "castles" from which the area takes its name date back as far as the 15th century, when they were built both as coastal defences and lavish retreats for the local nobles; you can walk from one to the next along the coast. The highlights are Kaštel Stari (the oldest), which has a decent stretch of beach, pretty Kaštel Gomilica, Kaštel Kambelovac, which has a seafood restaurant, and Kaštel Lukšić, which has been converted into a museum and is close to two beautiful gardens.

The waterfront at Trogir

2 Trogir Old Town

When you've explored the myriad churches, palaces and grand buildings of this perfectly preserved gem *(see pp28–9)*, relax on the wide waterfront Riva, where pavement cafés and alfresco restaurants bubble with activity day and night.

3 Makarska

MAP L4 ■ Tourist info. Obala Kralja Tomislava 16; 021 650 076; www.makarska-info.hr

The pretty port town of Makarska lies within a bay sheltered by the forested St Peter's Peninsula and is one of Dalmatia's liveliest and most popular mainland resorts. The historic centre is full of buildings that date back to Venetian rule, including the Baroque Church of St Mark overlooking the main square. Around the coast, the tone is more lively and modern. Two seafront promenades are lined with bars, restaurants and watersports-hire companies.

A sheltered bay at Makarska

4 Živogošće and Zaostrog

MAP E4 ■ Tourist info: Porat 87; 021 627 077; www.zivogosce.hr

At the southern end of the Makarska Riviera is the resort of Živogošće, which consists of three settlements: Porat, Mala Duba and Blato. Živogošće's highlight is its 17th-century Franciscan monastery, which has an impressive Baroque altar and a renowned library, with holdings that shed light on life during the Ottoman occupation of the region. Slightly further south is Zaostrog, home to an older (14th-century) Franciscan monastery with a small art gallery and folk museum.

5 Salona

MAP C3

Salona (derived from the Latin word for salt) is believed to be the birthplace of Emperor Diocletian *(see p33)*. Nowadays it's a ruin, with none of the life and energy of Diocletian's Palace, but this old Roman town just outside Split does allow visitors to gain an insight into ancient Roman life. Despite the surrounding industrial development, it's a pretty site, with mountains to one side and the Adriatic to the other. The Tusculum is a good place to begin your exploration. Also look out for the amphitheatre, the Roman baths, the Forum, the Theatre and the Necropolis of Manastirine.

LANGUAGE AND NATIONHOOD

Under French rule (1806–15), Croatian became the "official" language of Dalmatia, but when the Austrians took over in 1813, they re-introduced Italian as the language of public life – an important spur for the growth of Croatian nationalism. In 1865, Makarska became one of the first communes to bring back Croatian as its official language.

6 Gradac

MAP E4 ■ Tourist info: S. Radića 1; 021 697 511; www.gradac.hr

Gradac is best known for its beach, which at 6 km (4 miles) is the longest on the Croatian coast *(see p49)*. This spectacular spot has the Biokovo Mountains rising to the north and the islands of Central Dalmatia to the south. There's plenty of shade for the hottest summer days, as well as a campsites and hotels for those who fancy an extended stay.

7 Klis

MAP C3 ■ Tourist info: Trg Mejdan 10; 021 240 578; www.tvrdavaklis.com

This hulking fortress complex in the mountains above Split offers impressive views of the area. The Romans were first to use the site. Later it became a bulwark against the Ottomans, who finally captured it in 1537 after a bitter siege; they held it for more than a century, to the dismay of the residents of Split.

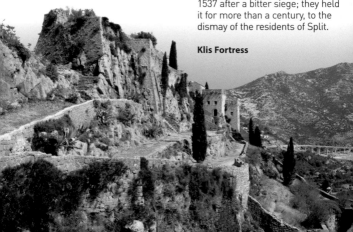

Klis Fortress

8 Diocletian's Palace, Split

Make sure you leave plenty of time to explore and relax in one of the most atmospheric city centres in Europe. The warren-like complex is so captivating that day-trippers often end up missing their ferry or staying an extra day or two. The palace *(see pp30–31)* is not at all how you expect an ancient monument to be; it's full of life, with people hanging their washing out of the windows of flats set into its walls, bustling restaurants, and funky bars where locals come to see and be seen.

Beautiful shingle beach at Brela

9 Brela
MAP D3 ■ Tourist info: Trg A. Stepinca 10; 021 618 455; www.brela.hr

Travelling south from Split, this is the first resort on the Makarska Riviera, and one of the nicest spots for a day or two by the sea. Brela is a pleasant town with a gaggle of old stone houses and a few modern hotels and restaurants, but it's the pebble and shingle beach that people flock here for.

10 Omiš
MAP C3 ■ Tourist info: Fošal 1a; 021 861 350; www.visitomis.hr

Set at the point where the Cetina river flows into the Adriatic, Omiš offers many outdoor adventures, including kayaking, canyoning, climbing, diving and rafting trips *(see p52)*. Once a notorious pirate stronghold, today Omiš is a largely modern town, although it does have a small historic quarter, and two fortresses – Mirabela and Fortica – that testify to its past of piracy.

THE ENVIRONS OF SPLIT

▶ MORNING

Head for the town of Solin, just outside Split, where the ruins of ancient Salona rise above the vineyards and fruit orchards. Don't miss the late Roman basilicas and the 2nd-century amphitheatre. It will take 50–75 minutes to walk the site, so take water and a hat in the height of summer. Grab refreshments in the café at the entrance to the Salona site before heading north to Klis, the 10th-century fortress that commands the high ground above Split. Take time to soak up the views from Klis's walls – ramparts that will be familiar to fans of the fantasy series *Game of Thrones* (as the city of Meereen).

Stop for lunch at the Perlica restaurant just north of Klis Fortress. It's famous for it's spit-roast lamb with spring onions.

AFTERNOON

Heading towards Solin, take the old road to Trogir, which passes through the coastal settlement of Kaštela *(see p87)*. A sequence of seven linked villages each with its own kaštel or defensive tower, Kaštela is great for a seaside walk, with a coastal path winding its way past small shingle beaches.

Continue to **Trogir** *(see pp28–9)* for a late-afternoon stroll round the medieval piazzas and alley-ways. Reserve at least half an hour for Trogir cathedral – its stone carvings make it an essential sightseeing stop.

A drink on Trogir's waterfront ● is the perfect way to end the day's exploration.

See map on pp86–7 ←

Beaches

1 Vodice Beach, Gradac
MAP E4

The longest of the Makarska Riviera's pebble beaches is the furthest south, at Gradac. Overlooked by the grey mountains of the Biokovo range, it's a stirring place for a swim.

Gradac on the Makarska Riviera

2 Žnjan, Split
MAP C3

East of central Split, Žnjan is a long pebble beach with cafés, restaurants and facilities for children. The walk from Bačvice to Žnjan along the coastal path (30 minutes) is lovely, whatever the season.

3 Kašjuni, Split
MAP C3s

In a semi-hidden cove below Marjan peninsula, this crescent of fine shingle is highly popular. It is a west-facing beach with views of Čiovo island and fine sunsets.

4 Bene, Split
MAP C3

On the northern side of the Marjan peninsula, just beyond the Špinut marina, Bene is a predominantly rocky beach backed by pines. It has good facilities for children.

5 Okrug, Trogir
MAP B3

Just 5 km (3 miles) southeast of Trogir, near the settlement of Okrug Gornji, this 2-km- (1-mile-) long shingle strip dubbed "Copacabana" is hugely popular in the summer. There's a healthy sprinkling of beach bars and watersports facilities.

6 Medena, Trogir
MAPB3

West of Trogir, this long stretch of shingle is backed by bars, restaurants and sports courts. Enjoy seaside walks here at all times of year.

7 Krknjaši, Veli Drvenik
MAP B3

Krknjaši Bay is a beautiful inlet with a shallow sandy bottom. There's a bar-restaurant here, and the bay is popular with yachtspeople, but it is still blissfully uncommercialized.

8 Makarska Beach
MAP D4

In the centre of Makarska, there is a beach, almost 2 km (1 mile) long, backed by a line of cafés, restaurants and hotels. There are plenty of sports facilities, too.

9 Bačvice, Split

A broad bay with a shallow sandy floor, Bačvice *(see p32)* has been a local family favourite. It is famed as the home of picigin, the Dalmatian game in which participants try to prevent a ball from touching the water.

10 Punta Rata, Brela
MAP D3

The Makarska Riviera is famous for its pebble beaches, and Brela's Punta Rata is one of the finest, curving its way around a promontory at the northern end of the resort. It is an excellent place for a paddle.

Punta Rata at Brela

Inland Excursions

1 Sinj
MAP C2 ■ Tourist office: Put Petrovca 12 ■ 021 826 352 ■ www.visitsinj.hr

A historic mountain town with several interesting churches, museums and fortresses, Sinj is home to the Shrine of Our Miraculous Lady of Sinj, the largest Marian shrine in southern Croatia and the focal point of many pilgrimage trails.

2 Cetina Gorge
MAP D3

This starkly beautiful gorge cuts through the heart of Central Dalmatia, before a rendezvous with the Adriatic at Omiš. It is increasingly popular with rafters, who often start near the town of Penšići. Foodies savour its fish restaurants.

3 Zadvarje
MAP D3

This village is a good spot for appreciating the beauty of the Cetina Gorge. Nearby, at the Gubavica Falls, the Cetina river plunges dramatically almost 50 m (164 ft) through the karst landscape.

4 Mosor
MAP C3

A mountain range extending between Klis and Omiš, Mosor attractively frames the Cetina river and a number of small villages. Explore it by car, or join the Croatian climbers tackling the barren Mosor Mountain.

5 Red Lake and Blue Lake
MAP E3

You cannot see the 300-m- (984-ft-) wide Red Lake (Crveno Jezero), near Imotski, from afar, since it lies in an inaccessible pit. The strange ochre hue of its waters comes from the landscape. It is possible, however, to get down to water level at its sibling, the Blue Lake (Modro Jezero), which takes on a contrasting colour. In summer, low waters reveal bizarre rock formations at this eerie spot.

6 Plitvice Lakes
Off MAP ■ 053 751 015 ■ Open times vary, check website ■ Adm ■ www.np-plitvicka-jezera.hr

The UNESCO World Heritage listed Plitvice Lakes are an oasis of limestone pools, lakes and waterfalls in a well-organized national park.

The breathtaking Plitvice Lakes

7 Krka National Park
MAP A1 ■ www.npkrka.hr

This spectacular conservation area beside the Krka river is usually entered just above the town of Skradin at Skradinski buk, where boat trips are available for visitors.

8 Biokovo Nature Park
MAP D3–E4 ■ www.pp-biokovo.hr

The jagged ridges of the Biokovo range form one of Croatia's most majestic areas of natural wilderness. Head to the Skywalk Biokovo, which offers stunning views.

9 Mostar
MAP G3 ■ Tourist office: 387 (0)36 580 275

This Bosnian city has a famous bridge (see p71) on the Neretva river.

10 Livno
MAP D2 ■ www.tourismbih.com

This southern Bosnian town is renowned for its tasty unpasteurized cheese, which is inexpensive here.

See map on pp86–7 ←

Cafés, Bars and Nightlife

Interior of Smokvica, Trogir

① Smokvica, Trogir
MAP B3 ▪ Radovanov Trg 9

Set in the shadow of the cathedral, this café-bar opens at 7am for espresso and keeps going until the early hours, by which time it has transformed into a buzzing live-music venue with an extensive cocktail menu.

② Luxor, Split
MAP N2 ▪ Kraj Sv. Ivana 11

In the heart of Diocletian's Palace, this popular café has an Egyptian-themed interior. There is outdoor seating in the summer.

③ Bačvice, Split
MAP N6

Located south of the centre of Split, this massively popular modern nightlife complex is set on the bay of the same name. There's a multitude of bars, cafés, restaurants and nightclubs to choose from.

④ Academia Club Ghetto, Split
MAP M2 ▪ Dosud 10

This atmospheric bar is a local favourite, attracting few tourists as it sits on the often-ignored upper level of Diocletian's Palace. It has a spacious courtyard for summer nights.

⑤ Deep, Makarska
MAP D4 ▪ Šetalište fra Jure Radića 5a

Deep is famed for its extraordinary setting: a tunnel-shaped cave with a beach at the front door. A friendly crowd enjoys eclectic dance-pop here.

⑥ Zinfandel Food & Wine Bar, Split
MAP M2 ▪ Marulićeva 2

Named after a grape variety, this centrally located bar takes pride in its wine selection. Settle in for the evening with a refreshing glass paired with Dalmatian dishes.

⑦ Pivnica Pivac, Makarska
MAP D4 ▪ Marineta 13

This seafront café-bar is one of central Makarska's most popular meeting points. The choice of beers is top-notch, with Croatian craft ales and international brands.

⑧ Teraca Vidilica, Split
MAP M5 ▪ Nazorov prilaz 1

Sweeping views of the city, port and the islands are seen from this café on the Marjan hillside. It is worth the hike on a sunny day just to sit back with a drink and take in the scene.

⑨ Romana, Makarska
MAP D4 ▪ Obala kralja Tomislava 21

This is one of the most popular pavement cafés on Makarska's Riva, offering a superb range of cakes and ice creams, as well as good coffee. It serves handmade chocolates, too.

⑩ Door Bar, Split
MAP C3 ▪ Put Trstenika 19

With its big outdoor terrace, this hotel bar is one of Split's best spots for coffee, drinks and people-watching. Order a Dalmatian wine in the evening.

The terrace at Door Bar, Split

Places to Eat

1 Bajamonti Pizza Steak & Fish House, Split
MAP L2 ▪ Trg Republike 1
▪ www.restoran-bajamonti.hr ▪ €€€
Located in one of the most attractive squares in the Old Town, this restaurant is popular among locals for its irresistible wood-fired pizzas, high-quality steaks and fish dishes.

2 Noštromo, Split
MAP L2 ▪ Kraj Sv Marije 10
▪ 091 405 6666 ▪ €€€
This smart seafood restaurant (see p56) is right by the fish market. Sit upstairs and watch as the ultra-fresh seafood is grilled in front of you.

3 Šperun, Split
MAP L2 ▪ Šperun 3
▪ 021 346 999 ▪ €€
Set between the seafront and hillside Varoš, this charming restaurant serves local specialities in a dining room filled with antiques and modern art. It's small but popular, so it can get crowded.

4 Restoran Riva, Trogir
MAP B3 ▪ Obala bana Berislavića 15 ▪ 091 582 5931 ▪ €€
Located in Trogir's Old Town, this restaurant has a terrace that overlooks the Riva. Open from April to November, it serves typical Dalmatian dishes.

5 Stari Mlin, Makarska
MAP D4 ▪ Prvosvibanjska 43
▪ 021 611 509 ▪ €€
Stari Mlin specializes in both Dalmatian seafood and fragrant Thai dishes, which go surprisingly well together. It is set in an old stone mill with a pretty walled garden.

6 Šug, Split
MAP N1 ▪ Tolstojeva 1A
▪ 099 458 8994 ▪ €€
Set outside the walls of Diocletian's Palace, this restaurant is popular with locals and serves modern Dalmatian fare, such as venison stew and seafood risotto. Book well in advance.

7 Villa Spiza, Split
MAP M2 ▪ Kružićeva 3
▪ 091 152 1249 ▪ €
Something of a cult restaurant among Dalmatian foodies, Spiza excels in traditional stews and seafood dishes, served in a tiny room. The menu changes daily based on what is fresh.

The patio at Baletna Škola, Kaštela

8 Baletna Škola, Kaštela
MAP B3 ▪ Don Frane Bege 2, Kaštel Kambelovac ▪ 021 220 208 ▪ €
On the seafront road, this restaurant enjoys a loyal following on account of its excellent seafood and inexpensive pizzas.

9 Bufet Fife, Split
MAP L2 ▪ Trumbićeva obala 11 ▪ 021 345 223 ▪ €
This long-standing local favourite serves hearty lunches – think traditional bean stews and inexpensive fillets of fish.

10 Kalalarga, Makarska
MAP D4 ▪ Kalalarga 40
▪ 098 990 2908 ▪ €€
Combining tradition with a taste for culinary daring, Kalalarga serves a trusted menu of fish, seafood and steaks with the odd innovative twist.

See map on pp86–7

⭐🔟 Southern Dalmatia

Meštrović sculpture at the Račić Mausoleum in Cavtat

Dubrovnik's popularity notwithstanding, Southern Dalmatia remains relatively unexplored and unspoiled. Its appeal lies in the diversity of the natural landscape, with pristine beaches, sheer cliffs, fertile farmland, dense forests, rolling hills and dramatic mountains all in one easily navigable strip of land. The Adriatic is not far away – the generous provider of the quality seafood served in even the most humble *konoba* (taverna). Expect excellent local wines from the vineyards of the Pelješac Peninsula here, too.

① Neretva Delta
MAP F5 ■ Tourist info: Brsalje ul. 5, Dubrovnik; 020 312 011

On its journey to the sea, the Neretva river fans out to create the lush, water-drenched landscape of the Neretva Delta. This 200-sq-km (77-sq-mile) expanse is partially navigable by boat, and can also be explored by car. Not only is the

The lush Neretva Delta

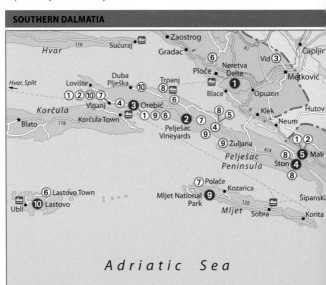

SOUTHERN DALMATIA

0 km 15
0 miles 15

Adriatic Sea

delta vital to Croatian agriculture, it provides a sanctuary for the myriad species of bird that stop off here as they migrate south to Africa. Many fish inhabit this angler's paradise, including eels and trout. The tourist information centre in Dubrovnik provides details on how and where to book a trip to the delta.

② Pelješac Vineyards
MAP E5

Many people treat the Pelješac Peninsula as little more than a quick route from Dubrovnik to Korčula town. In doing so, they miss an opportunity to explore the vineyards that produce what is arguably Croatia's best red wine, Dingač. A guided tour is a simple way of rectifying this oversight; Dubrovnik's tourist information centre provides information on tour providers. From Potomje, tunnels bored into the Pelješac mountains lead to quiet beaches.

The harbour at Orebić

③ Orebić
MAP E5 ■ Tourist info: Zrinsko-Frankopanska 2 ■ 020 713 718
■ www.visitorebic-croatia.hr

The small seaside town of Orebić, on the Pelješac Peninsula, has been attracting visitors for decades, with its idyllic location, long pebble beaches, and laid-back cafés and restaurants. The town's luxurious apartments are an alternative to the nearby hotels.

④ Ston
MAP F6 ■ Tourist info: Gundulićeva poljana 1 ■ 020 754 452
■ www.ston.hr

The Republic of Ragusa (see pp12–13) left an enduring reminder of its presence in Ston. The 14th-century fortifications, built to guard against attack by sea, resemble a miniature Great Wall of China. Today's relaxed pace of life is a far cry from the days when Ston was the second most powerful centre in the Republic. Other attractions include salt pans, and great views of the Dinaric Mountains and the peaks of Bosnia-Herzegovina.

Stolac

Trsteno Arboretum ⑥
Orašac ⑤④⑨ Komolac
ološep ⑤ 20 Trebinje
Dubrovnik Srebreno

BOSNIA & HERZEGOVINA

Cavtat ⑦
③⑤④ Čilipi ② Sokol grad ⑧
Gruda ⑩

Fortifications at Ston

⑤ Mali Ston
MAP G6

A short walk north of Ston is its smaller sibling Mali Ston. Gastronomes from all over Croatia and Italy flock to "Little Ston" for the finest fresh fish, with shellfish plucked straight from the Malostonski Channel seen as a highlight on any menu. The scenery is as spectacular as the seafood, and it is no surprise that this idyllic spot has become a popular haunt with Croatian weekenders.

⑥ Trsteno Arboretum
MAP G6 ■ Potok 20, Trsteno ■ 020 751 019 ■ Open May–Oct: 7am–7pm daily; Nov–Apr: 8am–4pm daily ■ Adm

At the end of the 15th century, the Gučetić family built a summer retreat overlooking the coast at Trsteno and gave it a beautiful Renaissance garden. The garden still survives in something approaching its original shape and has been expanded to form one of Europe's most impressive arboretums. This collection of trees and plants from around the world tumbles towards the Adriatic, with fine views of Trsteno harbour and the Elafiti Islands beyond. One of the highlights here is a water garden with an ornate fountain depicting Neptune surrounded by nymphs. The Arboretum is a unit of the Croatian Academy of Sciences and Arts.

NEUM

The road between Split and Dubrovnik passes through a 9-km (6-mile) stretch of coast owned by Bosnia-Herzegovina. Up until the Pelješac Bridge opened in 2022, visitors driving between the two Croatian cities had to stop to show their passports to officials. By connecting the Pelješac Peninsula, the bridge has made travelling along the coastline much easier.

Sculpture at the Račić Mausoleum in Cavtat

⑦ Cavtat
MAP H7 ■ Zidine 6 ■ 020 479 025 ■ www.visit.cavtat-konavle.com

First inhabited in the 3rd century BCE, this resort still bears the marks of the Illyrians, Greeks, Romans and Slavs who have occupied it. Look for the 16th-century Rector's Palace, and a mausoleum designed by Ivan Meštrović. Also worth a visit is Bukovac House, dedicated to the memory of one of Croatia's most famous painters.

Fountain at Trsteno Arboretum, with Neptune as its focus

⑧ Sokol grad

MAP J7 ▪ Dunave ▪ 020 638 800 ▪ Open Apr & May: 10am–6pm; Jun–Oct: 8am–8pm; Nov: 9am–3pm; Dec–Mar: 11am–3pm ▪ Adm

Overlooked by stark grey mountains, Sokol grad ("Hawk Castle") sprouts from a fist-shaped clump of rock. A fortress since prehistoric times, this was an important part of the Republic of Ragusa's frontier defences at times of Ottoman attack. This much-visited attraction has great views from its ramparts and a rewarding display of medieval military hardware inside.

Mljet National Park

⑨ Mljet National Park

MAP E6 ▪ Pristanište 2, Goveđari ▪ 020 744 041 ▪ www.np-mljet.hr ▪ Adm (children free)

The western corner of Mljet was designated a National Park in 1960 to conserve the island's holm oak and Aleppo pine forests. Among the main attractions are the intercon-nected saltwater lakes, Veliko Jezero ("Great Lake") and Malo Jezero ("Small Lake"). The islet of St Mary, in Veliko Jezero, is home to a 12th-century Benedictine monastery. Another highlight is the village of Polače, with its Roman ruins astride the harbour.

⑩ Lastovo

MAP D6 ▪ Tourist info: Pjevor 7; 020 801 018; www.tz-lastovo.hr

Reached by catamaran from Dubrovnik or the regular ferry service from Split, Lastovo is less visited than Southern Dalmatia's other islands. The main settlement, Lastovo town, is on a steep inland hillside, so many of its streets are akin to stone stair-ways. Zaklopatica bay has a couple of excellent seafood restaurants.

THE ELAPHITE ISLANDS

This itinerary is based on the summer ferry timetable (Jul & Aug), which makes it possible to visit three islands in one day. At other times of year, one or two islands is more realistic.

▶ MORNING

After coffee in one of the seafront cafés on **Gruž Harbour**, take the ferry to **Koločep** *(see p98)*, arriving at the island's small harbour 30 minutes later. You have a few hours before your next departure, which is plenty of time to explore the island's clifftop paths or loll on Koločep's smooth sandy beach. Opt for a lunch of squid or fish in one of the harbour-front restaurants, keeping a watchful eye on the arrival of your next ferry connection.

AFTERNOON

The afternoon ferry whisks you from Koločep to **Lopud** *(see p98)*, where you can stroll around the **Đorđić-Mayneri Park** *(see p61)*, take a peek at the **Church of Our Lady of the Rocks** *(see p44)*, and jump aboard a golf-cart taxi to the fabulous beach at **Šunj** *(see p99)*, before catching the ferry to Sudurad on the south coast of **Šipan** *(see p98)*. As soon as you arrive, amble around its attractive harbour and admire the fortified Renaissance villa of the Skočibuha family. Then, it's time for your final ferry of the day, which makes a leisurely journey along the South Dalmatian coast from Sudurad, arriving back in Dubrovnik just in time for dinner.

See map on pp94–5 ←

The Best of the Rest

1 Viganj
MAP E5

This small settlement with a 17th-century Dominican monastery unfolds around the Bay of Viganj, backed by the Pelješac mountains and looking out to the island of Korčula. Windsurfers flock to this picturesque spot for its reliably windswept beaches.

Performance in the centre of Čilipi

2 Čilipi
MAP H7

With regular folk events and an ethnographic museum, Čilipi is on the tour circuit from Dubrovnik. On Sundays during high season, the presence of performers in traditional costumes brightens up the main square.

3 Vid
MAP F5

Inhabited by both Greeks and Romans, Vid thrived as a trading post between the islands and the hinterland until the 7th century CE. View the remains of Roman Narona throughout the town, as well as at Vid's museum.

4 Janjina
MAP F5

This compact village, with an ornate church, tumbles down the Pelješac hillside towards the sea. It's a great place for wine from local vineyards.

5 Koločep
MAP G6

One of the Elafiti Islands, Koločep is mainly renowned for a sandy beach that is seldom as crowded as Dubrovnik's, a short ferry ride away. There are two small villages to explore, as well as the dense woods that cover most of the island.

6 Baćina Lakes
MAP F5

These six interlinked freshwater lakes just north of Ploče are an impressive sight. Surrounded by lush vegetation, they provide a habitat for a plethora of fish and bird species.

7 Lopud
MAP G6

Once a populous stronghold of the Republic of Ragusa, Lopud now enjoys a peaceful retirement. An old monastery, churches and a choice of beaches make this Elafiti island worth a visit.

8 Trpanj
MAP E5 ■ Tourist office: Žalo 7 ■ 020 743 433 ■ www.tzo-trpanj.hr

The Pelješac Peninsula's north coast is the picturesque setting for a small resort with a pebble beach and a cluster of pavement cafés. Trpanj affords sweeping views across Malo More towards the Biokovo Mountains.

9 Trstenik
MAP F5

On the south coast of the Pelješac Peninsula you can visit relaxed Trstenik, known for its old stone houses and sheltered harbour. Protected by the hills that rear up behind it, the village has seaward views of Mljet and Lastovo.

10 Šipan
MAP G6

The largest of the Elafiti Islands is also the richest in monuments, including both churches and fortresses.

→ **See map on pp94–5**

Beaches

1 Kupari
MAP H6

This crescent of shingle is one of the finest beaches in Dubrovnik, with crystal clear water and picturesque views.

2 Srebreno
Immediately east of Kupari, Srebreno *(see p71)* is a shallow semicircular bay bordered by boating piers and shingle beaches. There are cafés along the seafront and a luxury hotel looms just above.

3 Šunj, Lopud
MAP G6

This mixture of shingle and sand stretches across a bay on the eastern side of Lopud island, looking back towards Koločep and Dubrovnik. The path to Šunj from Lopud harbour takes you through some lovely untouched island scenery.

4 Koločep
MAP G6

A ferry ride away from Dubrovnik, Koločep has a small but pretty curve of sandy beach a short walk from the ferry harbour. There's a hotel behind the beach offering café, restaurant and beach-hire facilities.

5 Drače
MAP F5

With stretches of pebble spread either side of the small village harbour of Drače, the north-facing beaches of Drače offer splendid views of the mountainous Dalmatian mainland.

Pretty Divna beach, Trpanj

6 Trstenica, Orebić
MAP E5

One of the Pelješac Peninsula's most popular family beaches, Trstenica is a grand sweep of fine shingle with views of Korčula island. The beach is at the beginning of Orebić's seafront, which unfurls as you walk along the strand.

7 Punta, Viganj
MAP E5

A pebbly spit reaching into the Korčula channel, Punta is favoured by windsurfers but also has plenty of space for sunbathers and swimmers. Buzzing beach bars are just inland.

8 Papratno, Ston
MAP F6

Just 3 km (2 miles) west of Ston, Papratno beach is a long strip of fine shingle washed by warm, clear seas. There's a large campsite with plenty of eating and drinking facilities, and a nearby harbour for ferries to Mljet.

9 Vučine, Žuljana
MAP F5

A few minutes' walk from Žuljana village, this fine strip of pebble is surrounded by greenery and over-looked by steep, maquis-covered slopes. Facing west, it's a great place for sunsets.

10 Divna, Trpanj
MAP E5

You'll need your own transport to get to Divna, a secluded shingle beach at the end of a ravine west of Trpanj. You won't be entirely alone: there's a small campsite and a rudimentary beach bar for refreshments.

Bars and Wineries

The vaulted tasting room at Korta Katarina Winery, Orebić

1 Korta Katarina Winery, Orebić

MAP E5 ▪ Bana Jelačića 3 ▪ 099 492 5830

This winery just outside Orebić makes outstanding reds from its own vineyards and dry whites from grapes harvested in Korčula. There's also a wine bar, tasting room and shop.

2 K2, Viganj

MAP E5 ▪ Viganj bb ▪ Closed Oct–Apr

There's a day-long buzz at this open-air bar behind Punta Beach, often packed with windsurfers. Nights see a flurry of DJs and live music.

3 Vertigo, Srebreno

MAP H6 ▪ Dr F Tuđmana 20

Overlooking the sea, 10 km (6 miles) southeast of Dubrovnik, this popular spot is a café by day and a club by night. It has a range of guest DJs.

4 Riva, Cavtat

MAP H7

While away a pleasant hour or so at one of the café-bars on Cavtat's waterfront, taking in the distinctly Mediterranean ambience and the views over the bay and islands.

5 G Chelo, Koločep

MAP G6 ▪ Gornje čelo ▪ 020 414 616

A 30-minute ferry ride from Dubrovnik, this relaxing lounge bar offers delicious cocktails and beautiful sea views.

6 Saints Hills Winery, Trpanj

MAP E5 ▪ Oskorušno ▪ 020 742 113 ▪ Open 11am–5pm by appt ▪ Dinner from 7pm (booking essential)

This impressive winery in an old farmhouse also has a gourmet, reservation-only restaurant.

7 Skaramuča Wine Bar, Pijavičino

MAP E5 ▪ Pijavičino 7 ▪ 020 742 211

Located inland from Skaramuča's hillside-hugging vineyards, this accessible, roadside spot is the place to taste and buy the famous velvety wine.

8 Edivo Wine Bar, Drače

MAP F5 ▪ Drače 18

In the coastal village of Drače, this wine bar does things differently, serving wine aged at the bottom of the sea in bottles and amphorae. Those who scuba dive can visit the underwater cellar – otherwise, enjoy your glass above water in the bar.

9 Waterfront, Orebić

MAP E5

After a day on one of Dalmatia's best beaches (see pp48–9), unwind further in one of Orebić's waterfront cafés, with great views of Korčula.

10 Konoba Karmela, Viganj

MAP E5 ▪ Viganj 36

With a shady wooden terrace over the water, this restaurant-bar is popular with locals. Great for coffee, beer, wine or a light Dalmatian meal.

Restaurants

PRICE CATEGORIES
For a three-course meal for one with half a bottle of wine (or equivalent meal), taxes and extra charges.

€ up to €50   €€ €50-75
€€€ over €75

(1) Vila Koruna, Mali Ston
MAP G6 ■ Mali Ston ■ 020 754 999 ■ €

Arguably the best choice in a small town that features a number of first-class fish restaurants, Vila Koruna *(see p56)* is a must for seafood lovers. It is also a popular romantic spot.

(2) Kapetanova Kuća, Mali Ston
MAP G6 ■ Mali Ston ■ 020 754 264 ■ €€

Another popular Mali Ston restaurant, Kapetanova Kuća serves up mussels taken straight from the Malostonski Channel, grilled fish and Pelješac wine. The seafood risotto is divine.

(3) Bugenvila, Cavtat
MAP H7 ■ Obala dr. Ante Starčevića 9 ■ 020 479 949 ■ €€€

Bugenvila *(see p56)* offers imaginative Mediterranean cuisine, a laid-back ambience and superb service. The seasonal menu focuses on fresh seafood and creative desserts. Quite pricey, but well worth it.

(4) Vrgorac, Orebić
MAP E5 ■ Perna 24 ■ 020 719 152 ■ €

With wooden tables on a leafy terrace, and views across the sea to Korčula Island, Vrgorac serves excellent Dalmatian seafood and local wines.

(5) Kolona, Cavtat
MAP H7 ■ Put Tihe 2 ■ 020 478 787 ■ Closed Nov–Mar ■ €€

Operating since 1985, Kolona is known for its excellent grilled fish and attentive service. Over the years, innovative dishes have crept onto the largely Dalmatian menu.

(6) Augusta Insula, Zaklopatica Bay, Lastovo
MAP D6 ■ Zaklopatica 21 ■ 098 571 884 ■ Closed Nov–Apr ■ €€

One of the best restaurants on Lastovo, this is a hit with the sailing crowd, who can moor up outside and enjoy the exquisite seafood.

(7) Ogigija, Mljet
MAP F6 ■ Polače 17 ■ 020 744 090 ■ Closed Oct–Apr ■ €€

The emphasis is on fish at this pension and restaurant, which has a large terrace looking out over the sea.

(8) Bakus, Ston
MAP F6 ■ Angeli Radovani 5 ■ 020 754 270 ■ €€

Mixing traditional Dalmatian cooking with high culinary standards, this is the perfect spot *(see p56)* for local shellfish and some unique desserts.

Superb seafood at Bakus

(9) Gverović-Orsan, Zaton Mali
MAP G6 ■ Na ratu 7 ■ 020 891 267 ■ Closed Dec–Mar ■ €€€

This excellent little restaurant, just a short drive north of Dubrovnik, serves quality fresh seafood right by the Adriatic.

(10) Koraćeva Kuća, Gruda
MAP J7 ■ Gruda bb ■ 020 791 557 ■ Closed mid-Oct–mid-Apr ■ €€

Come here for locally sourced meat dishes cooked the traditional way – either roasted in an ember-covered pot or grilled over a charcoal fire.

See map on pp94–5

Streetsmart

Onofrio's Large Fountain, Dubrovnik

Getting Around

Arriving by Air

The Dalmatian coast has two international airports: one in Dubrovnik and one in Split. The island of Brač also has a smaller airport, close to the town of Bol, which is mainly used for charter traffic from Europe, especially during the summer season. Alternatively, fly to Croatia's capital, Zagreb, and pick up a **Croatia Airlines** connecting flight to Dubrovnik or Split from there.

Dubrovnik airport is located 22 km (14 miles) southeast of the city, just beyond the coastal town of Cavtat. Regular buses run from the airport into Dubrovnik, dropping passengers at the Ploče Gate, the main eastern entrance to the Old City, before proceeding to the bus terminal on Dubrovnik's western outskirts. Be aware that the pick-up location on the route towards the airport from Dubrovnik is different: buses stop near the cable-car station instead of the Pile Gate. Airlines flying to Dubrovnik from the UK include **British Airways** and a few budget airlines. Flights from London are direct year-round, but more frequent in summer.

Split airport is 20 km (12 miles) west of town between Kaštela and Trogir. There is a bus service from the airport to Split bus station. Among the European airlines flying to Split are British Airways, **easyJet**, **Jet2** and **Wizzair**.

International Train Travel

Dubrovnik does not have a railway connection. The nearest station is at Split, which is connected to the European rail network via Zagreb. There are at least daily rail services to Zagreb from several European cities, particularly those in neighbouring countries. Split's train station is in the centre of the city. Split is 4–5 hours from Dubrovnik by car or bus.

Buy tickets and passes for international journeys via **Eurail** and **Interrail**. Bear in mind that flying is cheaper when coming from further afield, especially in low season.

Domestic Train Travel

There are two main types of domestic trains in Croatia. The first is passenger, or *putnički*, which is generally slow and stops at numerous stations. The second is intercity, or ICN, which is faster and more expensive as a result. The entire network is run by **Croatian Railways**. Safety and hygiene measures, timetables, ticket information, transport maps and more can be obtained from the Croatian Railways website.

Tickets should be purchased at the station before boarding the train; tickets purchased on board might incur a surcharge. Some passengers, including over-60s, are entitled to discounted tickets.

Long-Distance Buses

International coaches connect Croatia with the rest of Europe. There are regular services from major German cities to Zagreb and coastal cities, covering the stretch from Rijeka to Split. Many Italian cities are also connected to Zagreb by coach. **Flixbus** runs various services into Croatia with the occasional coach from the UK, though journey times are long. Suitcases and larger rucksacks will need to go into the luggage storage compartments below the bus, and these are likely to incur a surcharge.

Croatia's domestic coach services are divided into intercity, which offer direct connections between the larger cities, and regional services, which provide connections between the smaller towns and the main cities.

Dubrovnik Bus Station is 2 km (1 mile) west of the centre at Kantafig. Buses 1A and 1B run from here to the Pile Gate, the main entrance to the Old City. The bus station is served by several daily intercity buses from Zagreb, Split and elsewhere in Croatia. There are also daily international arrivals from Bosnia-Herzegovina, Montenegro and Germany.

Split Bus Station, next to the train station, is another major transport hub, with daily arrivals from all over Croatia, as well as from a number of German and Italian cities.

International Ferries

Dubrovnik and Split are Dalmatia's main entry points for international ferries, although there are a number of seasonal crossings from Italy to the Dalmatian Islands.

Dubrovnik's ferry port is at Gruž, 4 km (2 miles) west of the Old City, to which it is linked by buses 1A and 1B. It is served by ferry from the Italian port of Bari one to four times a week from late March to late November. The crossing takes 8–10 hours and usually runs overnight, although there is often a daytime sailing once per week in high season.

Split's ferry port is next to the train and bus stations on the eastern edge of the town centre. It is served by **Jadrolinija** ferries from the Italian city of Ancona. The journey takes 10–11 hours and is served by two ferries a week between November and March, four ferries a week in August, and three ferries a week during the rest of the year. In summer there is also an 11-hour **SNAV** ferry from Ancona.

If you are aiming straight for the islands, Stari Grad on Hvar is served by Jadrolinija ferries from Ancona in August.

Domestic Ferries

With so many islands, ferries constitute a major part of Croatia's infrastructure. They make the islands accessible from the mainland while also cutting journey times by road. Ferry tickets can be bought in advance online or at ports.

The majority of ferries and catamarans are run by state-owned Jadrolinija. These ferries transport passengers and vehicles. Timetables and fare information can be found online. Note that some ferries only run in summer. **Krilo** operates fast catamarans between Split and Dubrovnik during summer only, with stops at several islands en route.

In the Split district there are connections between Split and the islands of Brač (Supetar), Korčula (Vela Luka and Korčula Town), Hvar (to Starigrad and Hvar Town), Šolta (Rogač), Vis (to the port of the same name) and Lastovo (to Ubli). There are connections between Makarska and Sumartin (island of Brač), between Ploče and Trpanj on the Pelješac peninsula, between Orebić and Dominče (on the island of Korčula) and between Drvenik and Sućuraj (on Hvar).

In the district of Dubrovnik, the main connection is between Dubrovnik and the island of Mljet (Sobra), while there are also small ferries running between Dubrovnik and the Elaphite Islands of Koločep, Lopud and Šipan.

DIRECTORY

ARRIVING BY AIR

British Airways
🌐 britishairways.com

Croatia Airlines
🌐 croatiaairlines.com

Dubrovnik Airport
🌐 airport-dubrovnik.hr

easyJet
🌐 easyjet.com

Jet2
🌐 jet2.com

Split Airport
🌐 split-airport.hr

Wizzair
🌐 wizzair.com

INTERNATIONAL TRAIN TRAVEL

Eurail
🌐 eurail.com

Interrail
🌐 interrail.eu

DOMESTIC TRAIN TRAVEL

Croatian Railways
🌐 hzpp.hr

LONG-DISTANCE BUSES

Dubrovnik Bus Station
MAP J8
■ Obala Ivana Pavla II 44A
🌐 autobusni-kolodvor-dubrovnik.com

Flixbus
🌐 flixbus.hr

Split Bus Station
MAP N6
■ Obala kneza Domagoja 12
🌐 ak-split.hr

INTERNATIONAL FERRIES

Jadrolinija
🌐 jadrolinija.hr

SNAV
🌐 snav.it

DOMESTIC FERRIES

Krilo
🌐 krilo.hr

Public Transport

The transport system within Croatia is efficient. Connections to the islands are good and, thanks to an extensive bus network, small towns can be easily reached.

When planning a journey the best place to start is the website of the transport company for the town or province you are in. In Dubrovnik, this is the **Libertas** city bus service. Public transport in the Split region is provided by **Promet Split**. Safety measures, ticket information, timetables, transport maps and more can be obtained online.

Travelling by Bus

As there are no trains along the coast, intercity buses provide the best means of getting around Dalmatia. Dubrovnik, Makarska and Split all have well-organized bus stations with timetable information and ticket counters. Smaller towns usually have a bus shelter beside the road – passengers boarding here pay the driver directly.

Each of the main islands has a local bus service. Dubrovnik is served by Libertas city buses. Services usually run until midnight (1am in summer). Single-journey tickets cost €1.73 from a kiosk or €1.99 from the driver. There is a bus from Dubrovnik to Split roughly every hour (with a journey time of 4–5 hours).

Apart from smaller towns, tickets for longer journeys are usually bought at the bus station, while those for public transport in the cities can be bought at a newsstand (kiosk) before departure. If you're travelling to the islands from the mainland, your bus ticket will automatically include the ferry fare.

Arriving by Road

Dubrovnik lies at the extreme south of Croatia, and getting here by road can be time consuming, whatever your point of departure might be. If you are travelling from or through Italy, use one of the Bari–Dubrovnik or Ancona–Split ferries. Otherwise, the A1 Zagreb–Split–Ploče toll motorway is the quickest option, although it ends 123 km (76 miles) north of Dubrovnik, and the final stretch involves a tiring but scenic drive on the winding coastal highway.

Driving Around the Dalmatian Coast

Croatia has some stunning stretches of road so it's worth seeing the country by car. A driving licence issued by an EU country is valid. If visiting from outside the EU, you may need to apply for an International Driving Permit. Check with your local automobile association before you travel.

If you encounter difficulties while driving around the Dalmatian Coast, emergency road services are provided by the **HAK** (Croatian Automobile Club), which can be reached 24 hours a day by dialling (+385 1) 1987. The service offers repairs (a charge will apply) on the spot or in a garage (subject to transport), the removal of damaged cars and transport up to 100 km (62 miles) distance. HAK also provides useful information on road and maritime traffic, motorway tolls, any temporary diversions, fuel prices, approximate waiting times at borders, possible alternative routes and general assistance for those travelling by car.

Note that no vehicles are allowed inside Dubrovnik's Old City except for delivery vans, which are given access for a few hours every morning. Streets elsewhere in the centre are narrow, parking spaces are hard to find, and the one-way system is trying for the first-time visitor. It is far better to leave your car at the parking garage at Ilijina Glavica, just uphill from the Old City, and walk to the Pile Gate.

The main highway (Jadranska magistrala) that runs up the coast from Dubrovnik to Split can be very busy, but it provides a scenic journey.

Cars are allowed on the major islands, but it is expensive to transport them there by ferry and often cheaper to hire a vehicle on arrival.

Rules of the Road

Cars drive on the right hand-side of the road and safety belts should be worn in both the front and back seats. Children must sit in the back. Cars towing caravans must not exceed 80 km/h (50 mph). Road signs are generally more or less identical to those found in the rest of Europe. Note that it is illegal to drive with more than 0.5 per cent blood alcohol limit in the blood.

Car Rental

Car hire firms such as **Avis**, **Hertz** and **Sixt Rent-a-Car** can be found at airports and railway stations. Drivers need to produce their passport, driving licence and a credit card with enough capacity to cover the excess. Most rental agencies require drivers to be over the age of 21 and to have an international licence. Book online in advance for the best deals. Beware hidden charges levied by small local companies.

Parking

As elsewhere in Europe, car parking is an ever increasing problem in most Croatian cities. Likewise, in many smaller coastal towns, parking is much reduced, with many seafront promenades closed to traffic through the summer season. Where indicated, a parking ticket must be clearly displayed inside the car's front windscreen. If you park in a no-parking area, your vehicle can be forcibly removed by officials.

Some hotels have parking spaces reserved for guests. If you are travelling by car it is worth checking this in advance.

Roads and Tolls

Croatia's motorways are regarded as among the safest in Europe. There are plans to extend the motorway further down the coast to Dubrovnik. On certain stretches drivers pay a toll (by cash or credit card). There is also a toll for the bridge to the island of Krk and the Učka Tunnel.

Taxis

Taxis are a convenient way to get around the cities of the Dalmatian Coast. In Dubrovnik, taxis can be used to shuttle between the Old City, the port at Gruž, and the hotels of Lapad peninsula and Babin Kuk. **Dubrovnik taxi** ranks are located outside the western and eastern entrances to the Old City. **Split taxi** ranks can be found at the train and bus stations, as well as on the seafront Riva.

Only accept rides in licensed, metered taxis and always confirm the price with the driver before getting in. It's generally expected that passengers will round up the final metered price in place of a tip.

Cycling

Hilly Dubrovnik and crowded Split are far from ideal destinations for the urban cyclist. It is a different story on the islands of the Dalmatian Coast, where there is easy cycling in the coastal towns, well-marked trails in the hinterland, and plenty of places to rent bikes.

Walking and Hiking

With a vast network of clearly way-marked footpaths both on the coast and further inland, the Dalmatian Coast is a fantastic destination for walkers and hikers.

Even on the islands, rural areas are fairly easy to reach and weather is generally pleasant. Ensure you have good hiking boots, plenty of water, a map and a compass – and stick to your route. Tell someone where you're going and when you plan to return.

Walking is also an enjoyable way to explore compact city centres such as Dubrovnik and Split, where most of the key sites are within a short distance of one another.

Practical Information

Passports and Visas

For entry requirements, including visas, consult your nearest Croatian embassy or check the **Ministry of Foreign and European Affairs** website. Citizens of the UK, US, Canada, Australia and New Zealand do not need a visa for stays of up to three months but, from 2024, must apply in advance for the European Travel Information and Authorization System **(ETIAS)**. Visitors from other countries may also require an ETIAS, so check before travelling. EU nationals do not need a visa or an ETIAS.

Government Advice

Now more than ever, it is important to consult both your and the Croatian government's advice before travelling. Visitors can get up-to-date travel safety information from the **UK Foreign, Commonwealth & Development Office**, **US Department of State**, the **Australian Department of Foreign Affairs and Trade** and the Croatian Ministry of Foreign and European Affairs.

Customs Information

You can find information on the laws relating to goods and currency taken in or out of Croatia on the website of the **Ministry of Finance Customs Administration**.

Insurance

We recommend that you take out a comprehensive insurance policy covering theft, loss of belongings, medical care, cancellations and delays, and read the small print very carefully. UK citizens are eligible for free emergency medical care in Croatia provided they have a valid European Health Insurance Card (EHIC) or Global Health Insurance Card **(GHIC)**. Visitors from outside the EU must arrange their own private medical insurance.

Health

Croatia's public health services meet the high standards of those elsewhere in Europe.

Emergency medical care in Croatia is free for all UK and EU citizens. If you have an EHIC or GHIC, present this as soon as possible. You may have to pay after treatment and reclaim the money later.

For those visiting from other areas, payment of medical expenses is the patient's responsibility. As such it is important to arrange comprehensive medical insurance before travelling. If your travel plans include extreme sporting activities, such as rock climbing and some watersports, make sure the policy covers rescue services.

In Dubrovnik, the **General Hospital** deals with walk-in patients and is also the site of the city's main Accident and Emergency department.

In Split, the same job is done by the **Clinical-Hospital Centre** at Firule.

Smaller towns and the larger Adriatic islands are served by a health centre (Dom zdravlja), which will deal with most minor complaints but will transfer you to Split or Dubrovnik in the case of a serious ailment.

Seek medicinal supplies and advice for minor ailments from a pharmacy (ljekarna) which can be identified by the green cross above the door. Pharmacies are usually open all day (8am to 8pm) or in the morning or afternoon, depending on the day. Although it is easy to find all the more common over-the-counter medicines in pharmacies without too much difficulty it is best to carry an adequate supply of any prescription medicines you may need. Some medicines are not known by the commercial names given to them in their country of origin, but by the active ingredients contained in them. It is useful if you can produce a prescription issued by your own doctor as proof that you are authorized to take a particular medicine.

For information regarding COVID-19 vaccination requirements, consult government advice.

Unless otherwise stated, tap water is drinkable.

Smoking, Alcohol and Drugs

Smoking is banned in all enclosed public spaces, as well as open ones such s bus stations and stadiums. There's a fine for smoking where you shouldn't. Drivers have 0.5 per cent blood-alcohol limit.

D

It's a good idea for visitors to carry ID, especially if driving. If you are stopped by the police and don't have your passport with you, the police may escort you to wherever it is being kept so that you can show it to them.

Personal Security

Croatia's crime rate is low. There is little street crime, although visitors should take the usual precautions in busy places to protect valuables from pick-pockets – particularly on public transport or in busy tourist areas. It is worth hiding your money and documents from view.

Police, fire brigade and ambulance services can all be reached by dialling the same **emergency number**. The number also covers the mountain rescue service (HGSS), which helps those who encounter difficulties while hiking or climbing in the Dalmatian high-lands, as well as a maritime rescue service that performs the same function for those at sea.

While the country holds conservative Catholic values, Croatians are generally accepting of all people, regardless of their race, gender or sexuality. Homosexuality was legalized in Croatia in 1977, and in 2015 Croatia was rated fifth in terms of LGBTQ+ rights out of 49 European countries. On the Dalmatian coast, same-sex beaches can be found in Hvar and Lokrum. However, despite the many freedoms the LGBTQ+ community enjoy in Croatia, acceptance is not always a given. Rural communities may be less tolerant of public displays of affection and same-sex couples travelling together. If you do at any point feel unsafe, the **Safe Space Alliance** pinpoints your nearest place of refuge.

Travellers with Specific Requirements

The old cobbled streets and ancient buildings of the majority of Croatia's towns and cities are ill-equipped for visitors with limited mobility. Many sights do not have wheel-chair access or lifts, however the situation is improving; some transport terminals in big cities are now wheelchair-friendly and public toilets at stations, airports and large public venues are usually wheelchair-accessible.

Travelling to the islands requires a degree of forward planning. Wheelchair access to the smaller passenger-only ferries and catamarans is problematic due to their narrow gangways, so you should enquire at the ticket desk as to which vessels are accessible.

Specific resources for sight-impaired and hearing-impaired travel-lers are rare, but the **Association of Organi-zations of Disabled People in Croatia,** or SOIH, provides information.

Time Zone

Croatia is on Central European Time (CET). The clock moves forward one hour on the last Sunday in March, and back one hour on the last Sunday in October.

Money

Croatia's currency is the euro. Major credit, debit and prepaid currency cards are accepted in many shops and restaurants, but certainly not all. Contactless payments are becoming more widely accepted but it is advisable to carry some cash. Cash machines are widespread in towns and cities; less so in rural areas. A tip of 5–10 per cent is customary if service is particularly good.

Electrical Appliances

Power sockets are type F, fitting two-pronged plugs. Standard voltage is 230 volts.

Mobile Phones and Wi-Fi

Wi-Fi hotspots are abundant in big cities. Cafés and restaurants are usually happy to permit the use of their Wi-Fi on the condition that you make a purchase. Wi-Fi is free in most hotels.

Visitors from the EU can use their devices without being affected by data roaming charges. Some UK networks have reintroduced roaming charges. Check fees with your provider.

Postal Services

The Croatian national postal service – Hrvatska Pošta, or **HP** – operates a network of post offices, with branches in all towns. For sending ordinary post, stamps (marke) can also be bought from newspaper kiosks. Unless airmail is specifically requested, postcards and letters are sent overland. Letters and cards can be posted at post offices or the roadside yellow post boxes.

Dubrovnik and Split main post offices are open 7am–8pm Monday to Friday, and 8am–3pm on Saturday. Smaller branches in Southern Dalmatian towns and on the islands have slightly shorter opening hours. In summer, some post offices in tourist resorts extend their opening times until 10pm.

Weather

Southern Dalmatia enjoys hot dry summers and mild dry winters. Temperatures can be very high in July and August, when sunscreen is imperative.

Beware of the wind in Dalmatia. A northerly gale sometimes results in the suspension of catamaran-ferry services, and speed restrictions on main roads.

Opening Hours

Shops are usually open 8am–8pm Monday to Friday, and 8am–3pm Saturday. These hours are often longer in summer, but some shops close for a few hours in the afternoon when temperatures are at their highest.

Banks are open 8am–5pm Monday to Friday (some as late as 7pm), and from 8am to 1 or 2pm on Saturday.

Many museums and galleries are closed at least one day a week, usually Monday.

Situations can change quickly and unexpectedly. Always check before visiting attractions and hospitality venues for up-to-date opening hours and booking requirements.

Visitor Information

Tourist information for the whole country is handled by the **Croatian National Tourist Board** (Hrvatska Turistička Zajednica, or HTZ), which has a website offering detailed visitor information. In addition, every town and city has an official tourist office, providing information on local sights, facilities and activities and, in many cases, will provide you with a free map. **Dubrovnik** and **Split City Tourist offices** are usually open long hours, seven days a week, in the summer season.

Additionally, **Dubrovnik County Tourist Board** covers much of the Southern Dalmatian coast, as well as Korčula island. **Split County Tourist Board** covers the mainland coast around Split, as well as Šolta, Hvar, Vis and Brač.

The **Dubrovnik Pass** offers discounts and money saving tips.

Trips and Tours

Walking tours are a good way of unearthing a city's hidden details; try **Dubrovnik Walking Tours** or **Split Walking Tour**.

For excursions from Dubrovnik, contact **Gulliver Travel**. From Split, both **Split Adventure** and **Go Adventure** organize day trips.

The Biokovo mountain massif between Dubrovnik and Split is difficult to explore unless you take a trip with **Budanko Travel** or **Safari Buggy Biokovo**.

To visit the Blue Cave on Biševo, book a trip with **Alternatura** or the **Blue Cave Agency**.

On Hvar, **Secret Hvar** and **Hvar Adventure** offer wine tasting, hiking, and tours of the island's historic hill villages. **Idi & Vidi** offers excellent cultural and gourmet tours of Brač.

Local Customs

Croatians are fairly conservative. Noisy or drunken behaviour is frowned upon. The conflict of the 1990s *(see p41)* is still recent, and many locals were affected. Read up before you go, and treat the subject sensitively. Note that many Croatians don't appreciate it being called a "civil war".

Responsible Tourism

Due to a lot of tourists visiting the Dalmatian Coast, some towns and cities now have local laws about how tourists should behave. Split, Hvar Town and Dubrovnik have introduced a fine for wearing swimwear in city centres. Many further rules relate to lessening your impact, including those that incur hefty fines in Split *(p30)*. In Dubrovnik, do not discard cigarette butts in public spaces or consume food and beverages around cultural monuments; and keep dogs on a lead.

Language

Croatian is the official language. English is commonly spoken and Italian and German are also widely used. Outside large towns you may encounter staff who have basic English or German.

Taxes and Refunds

VAT ranges between 13 per cent and 25 per cent. Non-EU residents are entitled to a tax refund on purchases over €98. To make a claim you must request a tax receipt and export papers when you purchase goods. When leaving the country, present these, along with the receipt and your ID.

Accommodation

Croatia offers a variety of accommodation to suit any budget. Prices are often inflated, and lodgings fill up quickly, during the summer season, so book in advance.

DIRECTORY

POSTAL SERVICES

HP
🔲 posta.hr

VISITOR INFORMATION

Croatian National Tourist Board
🔲 croatia.hr

Dubrovnik City Tourist Office
🔲 tzdubrovnik.hr

Dubrovnik County Tourist Board
🔲 visitdubrovnik.hr

Dubrovnik Pass
🔲 dubrovnikpass.com

Split City Tourist Office
🔲 visitsplit.com

Split County Tourist Board
🔲 dalmatia.hr

TRIPS AND TOURS

Alternatura
🔲 alternatura.hr

Blue Cave Agency
🔲 visbluecave.com

Budanko Travel
🔲 budankotravel.com

Dubrovnik Walking Tours
🔲 dubrovnik-walking-tours.com

Go Adventure
🔲 goadventurehr

Gulliver Travel
🔲 gulliver.hr

Hvar Adventure
🔲 hvar-adventure.com

Idi & Vidi
🔲 idiividi.com

Safari Buggy Biokovo
🔲 safaribuggy.hr

Secret Hvar
🔲 secrethvar.com

Split Adventure
🔲 splitadventure.com

Split Walking Tour
🔲 splitwalkingtour.com

Places to Stay

PRICE CATEGORIES
For a standard, double room per night (with breakfast
if included), taxes and extra charges.

€ up to €120   €€ €120–240   €€€ over €240

Luxury Hotels

Dubrovnik President Valamar Collection Hotel
MAP H8 ▪ Iva Dulčića 142
▪ 020 441 100 ▪ Closed
Nov–Mar ▪ www.valamar.
com ▪ €€€
Located close to the
Old Town and a few
metres from the beach,
this hotel is set on the
scenic Babin Kuk penin-
sula. All rooms have sea
views and amenities
include a wellness centre,
indoor and outdoor
pools and an award-
winning restaurant.

Sheraton Dubrovnik Riviera, Srebreno
MAP H6 ▪ Šetalište dr
Frana Tuđmana 17
Srebreno ▪ 020 601 500
▪ www.sheratondubrovnik
riviera.com ▪ €€€
This contemporary
boomerang-shaped
hotel rises above the
Srebreno bay, 10 km
(6 miles) southeast of
Dubrovnik. As well as
providing access to the
beaches of the Dubrovnik
Riviera, this hotel has
indoor and outdoor pools,
a state-of-the-art wellness
centre, excellent restau-
rants and views of some
gorgeous Adriatic sunsets.

Adriana, Hvar Town
MAP C4 ▪ Fabrika 28
▪ 021 750 200 ▪ www.
suncanihvar.com ▪ €€€
Situated right on Hvar
harbour, this intimate
hotel offers small but
superbly equipped rooms
decked out in lavender
tones. The spa facilities
are among the best on
the island, and there is
a small pool. The bar
has great views of the
harbour and is the
ideal spot to relax
over cocktails.

Excelsior, Dubrovnik
MAP H8 ▪ Frana Supila 12
▪ 020 300 300 ▪ www.
adriaticluxuryhotels.com
▪ €€€
With a seaside setting
overlooking the Adriatic
just steps away from the
Old Town, and a long
history of hosting royals
and celebrities, Excelsior
is by far the finest hotel
in Dubrovnik. It offers
scenic views, flawless
service, three restau-
rants, a glamorous spa
and a stone paved beach.

Grand Villa Argentina, Dubrovnik
MAP H8 ▪ Frana Supila
14 ▪ 020 300 300 ▪ www.
adriaticluxuryhotels.com
▪ €€€
Set among beautifully
manicured terraced
gardens overlooking
the Adriatic, the five-star
Grand Villa Argentina
is just minutes away
from the Old Town.
With exclusive waterfront
views, direct beach access
and a luxury spa, it's
the ultimate choice for
a pampering seaside
retreat in Dubrovnik.

Hilton Imperial Dubrovnik
MAP J8 ▪ Marijana Blažića
2 ▪ 020 320 320 ▪ www.
dubrovnik.hilton.com
▪ €€€
Blending modern comfort
and historic charisma,
this hotel has 149 well-
appointed guest rooms
and suites, plus leisure
and dining options,
including The Imperial
Bar and Lounge, and the
refurbished Imperial
Terrace, an indoor pool with
a sunroof and a health club.

Lešić Dimitri Palace, Korčula Town
MAP E5 ▪ Don Pavla
Pose 1–6 ▪ 020 715 560
▪ Closed Nov–Mar ▪ www
ldpalace.com ▪ €€€
In a complex of medieval
stone buildings, this boutique aparthotel's six
residences have funky
contemporary interiors.
Facilities include private
boats, a Michelin-starred
restaurant and a spa with
Thai and Ayurveda
therapists.

Park, Split
MAP N6 ▪ Hatzeov perivoj
3 ▪ 021 406 400 ▪ www.
hotelpark-split.hr ▪ €€€
Regarded as one of the
best hotels in Split, the
Park is just set back from
the waterfront at Bačvice. It
has modern rooms, friendly
staff and a restaurant that
has a palm-fringed terrace
looking out to the sea.

The Pucić Palace, Dubrovnik
MAP G9 ▪ Od Puča 1
▪ 020 326 222 ▪ www.the
pucicpalace.com ▪ €€€
Classical elegance and
history pervade every

aspect of this refurbished Baroque palace. It is also the only heritage five-star hotel within the Old City walls.

Villa Dubrovnik, Dubrovnik
MAP K9 ▪ Vlaha Bukovca 6 ▪ 020 500 300 ▪ Closed Nov–Mar ▪ www.villa-dubrovnik.hr ▪ €€€
Perched on the cliffs above the St. Jacob precinct, Villa Dubrovnik is 15 minutes away from the Old City. It offers great views of the Old City and of the Island of Lokrum. Experience unrivalled gastronomy and high-class leisure here.

Resort Hotels

Hotel Odisej, Mljet National Park
MAP E6 ▪ Pomena ▪ 020 300 300 ▪ Closed Oct–Apr ▪ www.adriaticluxury hotels.com ▪ €€
This charming hotel is set in the heart of Mljet National Park. The rooms are fairly basic and a bit dated, though the apartment is more luxurious. The hotel has its own beautiful stone paved beach, plus a bar and a restaurant, but the spectacular setting steals the show.

Amfora, Hvar Town
MAP C4 ▪ Ulica biskupa Jurja Dubokovića 5 ▪ 021 750 300 ▪ Closed Nov–Mar ▪ www.suncanihvar.com ▪ €€
The largest hotel in Hvar is staggering in its scale. Its plus points include welcoming staff, pleasant bedrooms, many with views of the Pakleni Islands (see p34), and diverse sports facilities, including a large pool

area, with cascading waterfalls, which is surrounded by gardens.

Bluesun Elaphusa, Brač
MAP C4 ▪ Put Zlatnog rata 46, Bol ▪ 021 306 200 ▪ Closed Nov–Apr ▪ www.bluesunhotels.com ▪ €€€
Backed by pine woods and overlooking the sea, this big, modern four-star hotel has 300 rooms, six suites, a range of sports facilities and a wellness centre. It lies just a 5-minute walk from Bol's stunning Zlatni Rat beach.

Bluesun Holiday Village Velaris
MAP C3 ▪ Put Vele Luke 10 ▪ 021 606 600 ▪ www.velaris.hr ▪ €
A group of three- and four-star hotels and villas occupying a wooded promontory west of Supetar, this is an ideal choice for a family holiday. It has many seaside activities, with a shingle beach on one side and a rockier area offering windsurfing and scuba diving on the other.

Croatia, Cavtat
MAP H7 ▪ Frankopanska 10 ▪ 020 300 300 ▪ www.adriaticluxuryhotels.com ▪ €€€
Located in a forest, this tranquil five-star resort has everything you need: secluded beaches, indoor and outdoor pools, hiking trails, a luxury spa and wellness centre, and restaurants and bars.

Issa, Vis Town
MAP B5 ▪ Šetalište Apolonija Zanelle 5 ▪ 021 711 164 ▪ www.vis-hoteli.hr ▪ €
This unassuming three-star lacks many of the

extras offered by other hotels but commands an idyllic location, with a pristine pebble beach immediately below. Boat-rental facilities and scuba-diving courses are available nearby, and most rooms come with views of Vis town's bay.

Kompas, Dubrovnik
MAP J8 ▪ Kardinala Stepinca 21 ▪ 020 300 300 ▪ www.adriatic luxuryhotels.com ▪ €€€
This four-star hotel overlooks the popular beach area of Lapad Bay. There's a modern spa centre offering beauty treatments, and the balconied rooms offfer stunning views.

Marko Polo Hotel by Aminess, Korčula Town
MAP E5 ▪ Šetalište Frana Kršinića 33 ▪ 020 726 100 ▪ www.aminess.com ▪ €€
With great views across the harbour and Korčula's walled Old Town, this four-star hotel has an outdoor pool, a wellness centre and a small pebble beach. Most of the 103 rooms have sea views.

Radisson Blu Resort & Spa, Split
MAP C3 ▪ Put Trstenika 19 ▪ 021 303 030 ▪ www.radissonblu.com/resort-split ▪ €€€
On the coast, 3 km (2 miles) east of Split's Old City, this hotel has smart, contemporary rooms and suites. There is also an outdoor pool, a pebble beach and a luxurious spa.

Valamar Meteor Hotel, Makarska

MAP D4 ▪ Kralja Petra Krešimira IV 19 ▪ 021 564 200 ▪ www.valamar.com ▪ €€€

This four-star hotel runs along Makarska's long pebble beach. Its unique ziggurat shape ensures that all of its rooms offer sea-views. With spa facilities, indoor and outdoor pools and a gym, this hotel is ideal for those who enjoy keeping fit while on their holidays.

Boutique Hotels

Bol, Bol, Brač

MAP C4 ▪ Hrvatskih domobrana 19 ▪ 021 635 660 ▪ www.hotel-bol.com ▪ €€

Situated close to the Zlatni Rat beach and few minutes from the sea and centre of Bol, this small hotel has a restaurant, bar, gym, sauna and outdoor pool. Some rooms have views of Vidova gora, the highest peak of the island of Brač.

Hotel Korsal, Korčula Town

MAP E5 ▪ Šetalište Frana Kršinića 80 ▪ 020 715 722 ▪ Closed Nov–Apr ▪ www.hotel-korsal.com ▪ €€

By the sea, just a 10-minute walk from the old town, this four-star family-run hotel has fifteen rooms and four luxury suites, plus a good restaurant with a waterside terrace.

Luxe, Split

MAP N3 ▪ Ul Kralja Zvonimira 6 ▪ 021 314 444 ▪ www.hotelluxesplit.com ▪ €€€

This modern hotel features a combination of bright purple fabrics and white surfaces and fittings. Close to Diocletian's Palace, the upper floors offer great views.

Marmont, Split

MAP L2 ▪ Zadarska 13 ▪ 021 308 060 ▪ www.dlhv.hr/hotels/marmont-heritage-hotel ▪ €€€

In a beautifully renovated 15th-century stone building in Split's historic centre, this four-star hotel has 21 rooms with smart decor and black marble bathrooms, plus a plush Presidential Suite.

Osam, Supetar, Brač

MAP C3 ▪ Vlačica 3 ▪ 021 552 333 ▪ www.hotel-osam.com ▪ €€

Perched above the seaside road that leads from Supetar harbour, this hotel offers smart and sleek rooms. Public areas are decorated in natural, minimalist colours. The restaurant offers an imaginative line in modern European-Dalmatian fusion, and the rooftop cocktail bar has outstanding views of the mainland. No children allowed.

Peristil, Split

MAP N2 ▪ Poljana kraljice Jelene 5 ▪ 021 329 070 ▪ www.hotelperistil.com ▪ €€€

Set in the heart of Diocletian's Palace, the Peristil has 12 individually styled rooms at the heart of Diocletian's Palace. The decor is light and elegant, and the friendly staff provide impeccable service. The restaurant, Tiffany, serves exceptional Dalmatian cuisine. Book room 304, or the one overlooking the Peristyle (see p30) that oozes grandeur.

Riva Marina, Hvar Town

MAP C4 ▪ Riva 27 ▪ 021 750 100 ▪ Closed Nov–Mar ▪ www.suncani hvar.com ▪ €€€

Right on Hvar harbour, just opposite the yacht berths, the Riva is one of the swankiest retreats on the island. The hotel was completely refurbished in Mediterranean villa style in 2022. It has 50 elegant rooms and suites – try to secure a sea-facing room for the best views. The emphasis of this hotel is on pure indulgence. There's also an on-site restaurant.

Villa Wolff, Dubrovnik

MAP J8 ▪ Nika i Meda Pučića 1 ▪ 020 438 710 ▪ www.villa-wolff.hr ▪ €€

This six-room boutique hotel offers pleasant rooms and attentive service. The waterfront restaurant, Casa, with its picturesque setting is perfect for dinner. Located just a few minutes drive from the Old City walls, the hotel has a wonderfully lush garden and promises great sea views.

Aminess Korčula Heritage Hotel

MAP E5 ▪ Obala dr Franje Tuđmana 5 ▪ 020 797 900 ▪ www.aminess.com ▪ €€€

This grand old hotel is a real period piece. It opened on the eve of World War I and has been refurbished to meld the splendours of the *belle époque* with modern facilities and furnishings. Right on the Old Town's waterfront with a palm-fringed café, it's the perfect choice for unwinding.

Prijeko Palace, Dubrovnik
MAP F8 ▪ Prijeko 22 ▪ 020 321 145 ▪ www. prijekopalace.com ▪ €€€

One of the Old City's more flamboyant former palaces provides a history-steeped home to this intimate hotel. Cosy, apartment-style rooms feature modern art on the walls and mini-kitchenettes in the corner. The restaurant serves outstanding food with a French-Dalmatian twist, and the cakes available in the downstairs café are superb.

Vestibul Palace, Split
MAP M2 ▪ Iza Vestibula 4 ▪ 021 329 329 ▪ www. vestibulpalace.com ▪ €€€

Located in the heart of Diocletian's Palace, the Vestibul, sits in a medieval stone palace that was built right on top of the emperor's former living quarters. The interior is a design masterpiece, mixing modern minimalism and straight lines with the exposed stonework of the original structure.

Small Hotels and B&Bs

Boutique Accommodation Mljet, Mljet
MAP E6 ▪ Goveđari 14 ▪ 098 285 697 ▪ www. boutiqueaccommodation mljet.com ▪ €

Some of the most romantic apartments in Dalmatia can be found in this re-stored schoolhouse in the village of Goveđari, on the border of the Mljet

National Park. The decor strikes the perfect balance between modern conveniences and traditional furnishings, and there is a variety of idyllic local walks for the taking.

Ostrea, Mali Ston
MAP G6 ▪ Mali Ston ▪ 020 754 555 ▪ www.ostrea.hr ▪ €

Framed by the sea and the Pelješac hills, the Ostrea is an attractive small hotel within the former home of its proprietors, the Kralj family. Modern art adorns plain walls in the tasteful rooms and suite.

Villa Carrara, Trogir
MAP B3 ▪ Gradska 15 ▪ 021 881 075 ▪ www. karara-ap.com ▪ €

In Trogir's UNESCO-listed medieval Old City, this cosy B&B has eight rooms, all with antique furniture, wooden floors and some exposed beams and stonework. There's also a small breakfast room with elegant, wrought-iron chairs.

Villa Neretva, Metković
MAP F5 ▪ Krvavac II ▪ 020 672 200 ▪ www.hotel-restaurant-villa-neretva. hr ▪ €

Right at the heart of the Neretva Delta (see pp94–5), this waterfront restaurant with rooms provides com-fortable accommodation. It is a good base for explor-ing this extraordinary waterscape and it also runs boat tours for guests.

Villa Varoš, Split
MAP M5 ▪ Miljenka Smoje 1 ▪ 099 215 9538 ▪ www.villavaros.hr ▪ €€

A nicely restored medieval stone building offering

neat double rooms and apartments this small family-run guesthouse is in the Varoš quarter, just 5 minutes' walk from Diocletian's Palace. The delightful neighbour-hood is replete with narrow alleys and small local restaurants. Nearby is restaurant Konoba Fratelli, run by the same family. It offers Villa Varoš guests a 20 per cent discount on food.

The Byron, Dubrovnik
MAP G10 ▪ Pobijana 4 ▪ 099 668 0145 ▪ www. thebyrondubrovnik.com ▪ €€€

Housed in a UNESCO World Heritage building behind the cathedral, this small boutique hotel has a unique location. Every room differs wonderfully in layout and character, and comes equipped with an en-suite bath-room, a kitchenette and air conditioning. Friendly hosts are always on hand to offer local tips to guests.

Hotel Villa Pattiera, Cavtat
MAP H7 ▪ Trumbićev put 9 ▪ 020 478 800 ▪ Closed Nov–Mar ▪ www.villa-pattiera.hr ▪ €€€

This renovated and resplendent historic villa is the birthplace of the Croatian opera star Tino Pattiera. Now a family-run boutique hotel over-looking Cavtat's harbour, it has 12 stylish and indi-vidually decorated rooms. The hotel's excellent restaurant, Dalmacija, serves splendid tradi-tional cuisine and has outdoor tables.

San Giorgio, Vis Town

MAP B5 ▪ Petra Hektorovića 2 ▪ 021 607 630 ▪ www.hotel sangiorgiovis.com ▪ Closed Nov–Mar ▪ €€

The Kut area of Vis town is the location for this small, family-owned hotel. The historic setting, large guest rooms, tranquil location and excellent seafood restaurant all ensure a very pleasant stay. Some rooms have views of the sea.

Boutique Hotel Stari Grad, Dubrovnik

MAP F8 ▪ Od Sigurate 4 ▪ 020 322 244 ▪ www. hotelstarigrad.com ▪ €€€

This intimate, nine-room and five-suite establish-ment is tucked away in a narrow street just off Stradun, the main thoroughfare. The hotel is housed in a 16th-century nobleman's home. The lovely rooftop restaurant provides prime views of the Old Town and Adriatic Sea.

Budget

Biličić Guesthouse, Dubrovnik

Off MAP ▪ Privežna 2 ▪ 020 417 152 ▪ €

Cosy en-suite rooms and a lovely walled garden mark this out as one of the prettiest guesthouses in the city. It's situated just up the hill from Dubrovnik's walls, and the stroll down into the Old City is a great way to start the day. This is quite a popular place to stay, so be sure to book well in advance.

City Walls Hostel, Dubrovnik

MAP F10 ▪ Svetog Šimuna 15 ▪ 091 416 1919 ▪ www. citywallshostel.com ▪ Closed Nov–Mar ▪ €

Based in an old stone building near Dubrovnik's seaward walls, this place is popular with backpackers. It offers dormitory rooms with air conditioning, complimentary breakfast, a communal kitchen and free internet access to all.

Dvor, Split

MAP L2 ▪ Radmilovića 71 ▪ 021 785 908 ▪ www. hosteldvor.com ▪ €

This hostel has 13 rooms, from six-bed dorms to three private rooms. Every room is equipped with air conditioning, satellite TV and free Wi-Fi, but only some offer an en-suite bathroom.

The White Rabbit, Hvar Town

MAP B4 ▪ Stjepana Papafave 6 ▪ 021 717 365 ▪ www.greenlizard.hr ▪ Closed Oct–Apr ▪ €

A five-minute walk from the harbour, this centrally located hostel is a lively spot with bright, air con-ditioned rooms. Choose from 10 rooms – some of which are female-only – that range from eight-bed dorms to doubles. All guests have access to a convenient shared kitchen and free Wi-Fi.

Hostel Makarska, Makarska

MAP D4 ▪ Prvosvibanjska 15 ▪ 091 256 7212 ▪ www.hostelmakarska. com ▪ €

Located on one of central Makarska's narrow streets, this converted family house offers a

mixture of dormitory beds, private double rooms and family-sized self-catering apartments. Its location in a palm-shaded garden provides an extra touch of magic.

Marinero Hostel, Hvar Town

MAP C4 ▪ Put svetog Marka 7 ▪ 091 410 2751 ▪ www.hostel-marinero-hr.book.direct ▪ €

This tall and narrow stone house just around the corner from the harbour features airy dorm rooms with bunk beds. The ground floor is occupied by a restaurant, with rows of outdoor benches that are great for big groups. With neighbouring alleys packed with bars and food outlets, it's the kind of location that suits late-to-bed types.

Old Town Hostel, Dubrovnik

MAP F8 ▪ Od Sigurate 7 ▪ 020 322 007 ▪ www. dubrovnikoldtown hostel.com ▪ Closed Dec–Feb ▪ €

This hostel in a pretty Baroque stone building has eight rooms and can accommodate 25 guests. All rooms are white-washed, with wooden floors and old-fashioned bunk beds. There's also a kitchen and a common room with a TV. No air con

Vila Micika, Dubrovnik

MAP J8 ▪ Mata Vodopića 10 ▪ 098 243 717 ▪ www. vilamicika.hr ▪ €

Simple accommodation is on offer here in a typical Dalmatian stone villa in Lapad. There are just eight bedrooms, so book well in advance. All rooms are equipped with air conditioning and free Wi-Fi, and the villa also has a car park, a barbecue and a communal terrace.

Campsites

Antony Boy, Viganj
MAP E5 ▪ Viganj ▪ 020 719 077 ▪ www.antony-boy.com ▪ €

A level site partly shaded by olive trees, Antony Boy is right next to Viganj's pebbly Punta beach, which has become something of a haven for European windsurfers. The site itself comes with windsurf hire and a windsurf school and it also hires bikes to those who want to explore the semi-abandoned villages just inland.

Camping Grebišče, Jelsa
MAP C4 ▪ Grebišće ▪ 021 761 191 ▪ www.grebisce. hr ▪ Closed Nov–Apr ▪ €

Few campsites are better placed for an untroubled beach holiday than Hvar's Grebišće, which occupies a grassy bluff directly above Grebišće beach, a famously shallow bay that is sandy underfoot and perfect for kids. The centre of Jelsa is about 1.5 km (1 mile) to the west – ideal for a walk or a pleasant drive or cycle.

Camping Stobreč, Split
MAP C3 ▪ Sv Lovre 6 ▪ Stobreč, Split ▪ 021 325 426 ▪ www.campingsplit. com ▪ €

This well-equipped site at the eastern edge of town, 6 km (4 miles) from the centre, is perfectly placed beside the main road towards the Makarska Riviera. It has its own stretch of seafront and is

also well positioned for the long pebble beach at Žnjan, one of Split's most popular family destinations.

Camping Trsteno, Trsteno
MAP G6 ▪ Trsteno ▪ 020 751 060 ▪ Closed mid-Oct–Mar ▪ www.trsteno. hr ▪ €

Located up the hill from the Trsteno Arboretum, this pleasant, small-scale campsite is situated amid olive groves. Stairs lead to a pebble beach. On-site facilities include a shop and a restaurant.

Camp Makarska, Makarska
MAP D4 ▪ Ivana Gorana Kovačića ▪ 099 216 9871 ▪ www.camp-makarska. com ▪ €

At the entrance to Makarska, superbly located if visiting from Split, is this large site surrounded by a pine forest. It's home to seven apartments, five luxury mobile homes and 14 camping lots, as well as a sports recreation centre – a great spot for tennis or mini golf. Nearby is a pebble beach and superb bars and restaurants.

Camp Vira, Hvar Town
MAP C4 ▪ Vira ▪ 021 750 900 ▪ www.campvira.com ▪ Closed Oct–Apr ▪ €

Occupying its own bay 4 km (2 miles) from Hvar town, Vira runs behind a beautiful pebble beach, with pitches for caravans and tents set out on a terraced, pine-shaded slope. Kayaks can be hired on the beach, activities are organized for kids, and there is a bar-restaurant on site.

Camp Riviera, Makarska
MAP D4 ▪ Rosseto Degli Abruzzi 10 ▪ 021 549 542 ▪ www.campriviera.eu ▪ €

Camp Riviera offers the best of both worlds; it is set in a peaceful pine forest near the beach, but is also just 2 km (1 mile) away from central Makarska. The well-equipped site includes 120 pitches and a bar serving food and drinks.

Port 9 Campsite by Aminess, Korčula Town
MAP E5 ▪ Dubrovačka cesta 19 ▪ 020 726 801 ▪ Closed Oct–May ▪ www.aminess-campsites.com ▪ €

Just 2 km (1 mile) from the historic centre of Korčula town and 50 m (165 ft) from a beach, this campsite has 124 pitches. The facilities include a shop and a restaurant. There is a small extra charge for parking. Reduced rate for under-12s.

Solitudo Sunny Camping
MAP J8 ▪ Vatroslava Lisinskog 60 ▪ 020 448 686 ▪ Closed Nov–Mar ▪ www.camping-adriatic. com ▪ €

The only campsite in Dubrovnik, Solitudo Sunny Camping is located on the quiet wooded peninsula of Babin Kuk, just a ten-minute ride from the Old Town. It's an excellent starting point to explore Southern Dalmatia's historic and natural attractions. The pitches are shaded with pines, and caravans are also available. Free Wi-Fi.

For a key to hotel price categories see p112

General Index

Page numbers in **bold** refer to main entries

Acknowledgments

This edition updated by

Contributor Natasa Novakovic
Senior Editors Dipika Dasgupta, Zoë Rutland
Senior Art Editor Vinita Venugopal
Project Editor Anuroop Sanwalia
Project Art Editor Bharti Karakoti
Assistant Editor Ishita Chatterjee
Picture Research Administrator
Vagisha Pushp
Picture Research Manager Taiyaba Khatoon
Publishing Assistant Simona Velikova
Jacket Designer Jordan Lambley
Senior Cartograper Subhashree Bharati
Cartography Manager Suresh Kumar
DTP Designer Rohit Rojal
Senior Production Editor Jason Little
Production Controller Kariss Ainsworth
Managing Editors Shikha Kulkarni,
Beverly Smart, Hollie Teague
Senior Managing Art Editor Priyanka Thakur
Art Director Maxine Pedliham
Publishing Director Georgina Dee

DK would like to thank the following for their contribution to the previous editions:
Robin and Jenny McKelvieare, Jonathan Bousfield, the Croatian National Tourist Board, Clare Peel, Hilary Bird

The publisher would like to thank the following for their kind permission to reproduce their photographs:
Key: a-above; b-below/bottom; c-centre; f-far; l-left; r-right; t-top

123RF.com: Andrey Bodrov 71b.

Alamy Stock Photo: The Art Archive / Gianni Dagli Orti 33bl; Ivan Batinic 22br; Stephen Coyne 94tl; DustyDingo 54t; Alexei Fateev 95tr; funkyfood London - Paul Williams 6cr, 24–5; Ian Furniss 62bl; hemis.fr / Rene Mattes 47tr; imageBROKER / Günter Flegar 21b, 38–9, / Günter Lenz 47cl; Ingolf Pompe 41 4t; Bjanka Kadic 46tl, 96c; Justin Kase zsixz 60tr; LatitudeStock 98cla; Nino Marcutti 52br, 91cr; Itsik Marom 58tr; Odyssey-Images 51cl; Panama 40bc; photisca 51tr; Pixel 8 21tl; Dave Porter 21bl; Bart Pro 52bl; Michael Robertson 55tr; traveler 4cr; Travelfile 4b, 35bl; V&A Images 40cc; Scott Wilson 8-9; ZUMA Press, Inc. 63cl; Piotr Zadroga 61tr.

AWL Images: Alan Copson 1, Sabine Lubenow 53cl.

Bugenvila Cavtat: 56tl.

Club Lazareti: Fjaka 73cr.

Corbis: Bettmann 33cl.

Croatian National Tourist Board: Ivo Biocina 18cla; Aleksandar Gospić 23crb; Studio Gobbo 32bl.

D'Vino Wine Bar: 74tl.

Dorling Kindersley: Courtesy of the Galerija Meštrović, Muzeji Ivana Meštrovića / Lucio Rossi 46cb.

Dreamstime.com: Ailenn 68c; Mila Atkovska 15crb; Baloncici 10cl; Artur Bogacki 69tl; Olena Buyskykh 10cla; Ccat82 4cl; Mario Čehulić 86tl; Marilyn Ching 96b; Daniel M. Cisilino 11crb, 12c, 14cla, 14–15, 67tr; Sorin Colac 2tl, 8–9; Andras Csontos 7tl; Dbajurin 78bl; Dreamer4787 66cr; Donyanedomam 11bl; Stefano Ember 11cra; Luisa Vallon Fumi 28cla; Artur Gabrysiak 14bl; Janos Gaspar 68b, 89cl; Inavanhateren 66cla, 76tl, 81cr; Ivansmuk 59cl; Jarnogz 30bl; Jasmina 12–13, 13b, 36–7, 49tl, 50br; Joymsk 29bl; Kemaltaner 30br; Aleksandrs Kosarevs 12bl; Jan Krasa 26br; Landd09 54br, 60b; Lianem 90tl, 94cr; Lukaszimilena 7br, 11br, 36br; Marcinknop 95br; Mareticd 78tr, 81tl; Marinv 55cl; Galina Mikhalishina 4crb; Evgeniya Moroz 34bl; Mrakhr 22clb; Mtr 20–21; Nadtochiy 31tl; Nevenm 57tr; Nightman1965 12cla; Phant 10crb, 26–7; Saša Prijić 43cr; Reddogs 15ca; Rndmst 36cl, 44tl; Salajean 28bl; Sjankauskas 3tr, 102–3; Nikolai Sorokin 11c, 61cl; Kiril Stanchev 88b; Paula Stanley 45tc; Serghei Starus 84–5; Aleksandar Todorovic 27crb; Tuomaslehtinen 10bl, 20clb, 48cl; Vesnyanka 37br; Birute Vijeikiene 30-1c; Xbrchx 3tl, 11tl, 22–3, 26cl, 28–9, 31cr, 32t, 34–5, 42tl, 42b, 49b, 64–5, 77t, 79cl, 80b, 87tr.

Gaixa Hvar: Damir Fabijanic 83cl.

Getty Images: AFP PHOTO / Andrej Isakovic 53tr; Archive Photos / Buyenlarge 41cla; OGphoto 18–19.

Hula Hula Hvar Town: Marko Delbello Ocepek 82tl.

Ivana Bareta: 92tl.

Irish Pub "The Gaffe": 74br.

Konobia Adio Mare: 57cl.

Korta Katarina Winery: 100t.

Mediterranean Film Festival: 62tr.

Medusa: Tinka 72bl.

Oyster & Sushi Bar Bota: 75cra.

Punta Rata Beach, Brela: 90br.

Radisson Blu Resort & Spa, Split/ The Door Bar: 92br.

Restaurant Nautika: 56br.

Restoran Baletna Škola: 93cr.

Rex by Shutterstock: imageBROKER / Günter

Flegar 50t; SIPA / CROPIX / Zvonimir Barisin 53tr; SIPA PRESS 41clb, 41br.

Robert Harding Picture Library: Gonzalo Azumendi 70tl; Gunter Flegar 97cl; LOOK Bildagentur der Fotografen / Konrad Wothe 87br; Martin Moxter 18bl; Bernd Rohrschneider 45bl; Martin Siepmann 4clb; Matthew Williams-Ellis 4cla, 34crb.

Studio Magenta: Bakus Restaurant 101cr.

SuperStock: Mauritius / Wolfgang Weinhäupl 58bl; Prisma / Album 17br.

Trpanj Tourist Board: 99b

Uje: 59tr.

Cover

Front and spine, **AWL Images:** Alan Copson.

Back. **AWL Images:** Alan Copson b, Doug Pearson tr; **Dreamstime.com:** Oriontrail cla, Rudi1976 crb, Xbrchx tl.

Pull Out Map Cover

AWL Images: Alan Copson.

All other images © Dorling Kindersley

For further information see: www.dkimages.com

DK Penguin Random House

First Edition 2006

First published in Great Britain by Dorling Kindersley Limited DK, One Embassy Gardens, 8 Viaduct Gardens, London, SW11 7BW, UK

The authorised representative in the EEA is Dorling Kindersley Verlag GmbH. Arnulfstr. 124, 80636 Munich, Germany

Published in the United States by DK US, 1745 Broadway, 20th Floor, New York, NY 10019, USA

Copyright © 2006, 2024 Dorling Kindersley Limited

A Penguin Random House Company

23 24 25 26 10 9 8 7 6 5 4 3 2 1

All rights reserved.

No part of this publication may be reproduced, stored in or introduced into a retrieval system, or transmitted in any form, or by any means (electronic, mechanical, photocopying, recording or otherwise) without the prior written permission of the copyright owner.

The publishers cannot accept responsibility for any consequences arising from the use of this book, nor for any material on third party websites, and cannot guarantee that any website address in this book will be a suitable source of travel information.

A CIP catalogue record is available from the British Library.

A catalogue record for this book is available from the Library of Congress

ISSN 1479 344X

ISBN 978-0-2416-6495-7

Printed and bound in Malaysia

www.dk.com

As a guide to abbreviations in visitor information blocks: ***Adm*** *= admission charge;* ***D*** *= dinner.*

FSC www.fsc.org MIX Paper | Supporting responsible forestry FSC™ C018179

This book was made with Forest Stewardship Council™ certified paper – one small step in DK's commitment to a sustainable future.
For more information go to www.dk.com/our-green-pledge

Phrase Book

Pronunciation Guide

c – "ts" as in rats	č – "ch" as in church
ć – "t" is a soft t	đ – "d" as in endure
g – "g" as in get	j – "y" as in yes
š – "sh" as in shoe	ž – "J" as in Jacques
aj – "igh" as in night	

In an Emergency

Help!	Pomoć!	pomoch!
Stop!	Stani!	stahnee!
Call a doctor!	Zovite doktora!	zoveetey doktorah!
Call an ambulance!	Zovite hitnu pomoć!	zoveetey heetnoo pomoch!
Call the police!	Zovite policiju!	zoveetey poleetseeyoo!
Call the fire brigade!	Zovite vatrogasce!	zoveetey vatrohgastsay!

Communication Essentials

Yes	Da	dah
No	Ne	ney
Please	Molim vas	moleem vas
Thank you	Hvala	hvahlah
Excuse me	Oprostite	oprosteetey
Hello	Dobar dan	dobar dan
Goodbye	Doviđenja	doveedjenya
Good night	Laku noć	lakoo noch
Yesterday	Jučer	yoocher
Today	Danas	danas
Tomorrow	Sutra	sootrah
Here	Tu	too
There	Tamo	tahmoh
What?	Što?	shtoh
When?	Kada?	kada
Why?	Zašto?	zashtoh
Where?	Gdje?	gdyey

Useful Phrases

How are you?	Kako ste?	kakoh stey
Very well, thank you	Dobro, hvala	dobroh, hvahlah
Where is/are...?	Gdje je/su?	gdyey yey/soo?
How can I get to...?	Kako mogu doći do...?	kakoh mogoo dochee doh...
Do you speak English?	Govorite li engleski?	govoreetey lee engleskee?
I don't understand	Ne razumijem	nay razoomeeyem
Could you speak more slowly please?	Molim vas, možete li govoriti sporije?	moleem vas, mozhetey lee govoreetee sporiyey?
I'm sorry	Žao mi je	zhaoh mee yey

Useful Words

big	veliko	veleekoh
small	malo	mahloh
hot	vruć	vrooch
cold	hladan	hlahdan
good	dobar	dobar
bad	loš	losh
open	otvoreno	otvohrenoh
closed	zatvoreno	zatvohrenoh
left	lijevo	leeyevoh
right	desno	desnoh
straight on	ravno	ravnoh
near	blizu	bleezoo
far	daleko	dalekoh
up	gore	gorey

down	dolje	dolyey
early	rano	ranoh
late	kasno	kasnoh
entrance	ulaz	oolaz
exit	izlaz	eezlaz
toilet	WC	Vey tsey
more	više	veeshey
less	manje	manyey

Shopping

How much does this cost?	Koliko ovo košta?	kolikoh ovoh koshta?
I would like...	Volio bih...	volioh bee...
Do you have...?	Imate li...?	eematey lee...?
I'm just looking	Samo gledam	Samoh gledam
Do you take credit cards?	Primate li kreditne kartice?	preematey lee credeetney carteetsey?
What time do you open/close?	Kad otvarate/ zatvarate?	kad otvaratey/ zatvaratey?
This one	Ovaj	ov-igh
That one	Onaj	on-igh
expensive	skupo	skoopoh
cheap	jeftino	yefteenoh
size (clothes)	veličina	veleechinah
size (shoes)	broj	broy
white	bijelo	beeyeloh
black	crno	tsrnoh
red	crveno	tsrvenoh
yellow	žuto	zhootoh
green	zeleno	zelenoh
blue	plavo	plavoh
bakery	pekara	pekarah
bank	banka	bankah
book shop	knjižara	knyeezharah
butcher's	mesnica	mesnitsah
cake shop	slastičarna	slasteecharnah
chemist's	apoteka	apohtekah
fishmonger's	ribarnica	reebarnitsah
market	tržnica	trzhneetsah
hairdresser's	frizer	freezer
newsagent's	kiosk	keeosk
post office	pošta	poshtah

Sightseeing

art gallery	galerija umjetnina	galereeyah oomyetneenah
cathedral	katedrala	katedralah
church	crkva	tsrkvah
library	knjižnica	knyeezhneetsah
museum	muzej	moozey
tourist information centre	turistički ured	tooreesteechkey oored
bus station	autobusni kolodvor	aootoboosnee kolodvor
railway station	željeznički kolodvor	zhelyeznichkih kolodvor

Staying in a Hotel

Do you have a vacant room?	Imate li sobu?	eematey lee soboo
double room	dvokrevetna soba	dvokrevetnah sobah
single room	jednokrevetna soba	yednokrevetnah sobah
room with a bath	soba sa kupaonicom	sobah sah koopaoneetsom
shower	tuš	toosh
I have a reservation	Imam rezervaciju	eemam rezervatseeyoo

Eating Out

Have you got a table for...?	Imate li stol za...?	eematey lee stol zah
want to reserve a table	Želim rezervirati stol	Zheleem rezerveeratee stol
The bill please	Molim vas, račun	moleem vas, rachoon
I am a vegetarian	Ja sam vegetarijanac	yah sam vegetareeyanats
waiter/waitress	konobar/ konobarica	konobar/ konobaritsah
menu	jelovnik	yelovneek
wine list	vinska karta	veenskah kartah
glass	čaša	chashah
bottle	boca	botsah
knife	nož	nozh
fork	vilica	veeleetsa
spoon	žlica	zhleetsah
breakfast	doručak	doroochak
lunch	ručak	roochak
dinner	večera	vecherah
main course	glavno jelo	glavnoh yeloh
starters	predjela	predyelah

Menu Decoder

bijela riba	beeyelah reebah	"white" fish
blitva	bleetvah	Swiss chard
brudet	broodet	fish stew
ćevapčići	chevapcheechee	meatballs
crni rižot	tsrnee reezhot	black risotto
desert	desert	dessert
glavno jelo	glavnoh yeloh	main course
grah	grah	beans
gulaš	goolash	goulash
jastog	yastog	lobster
juha	yoohah	soup
kuhano	koohanoh	cooked
maslinovo ulje	masleenovoh oolyey	olive oil
meso na žaru	mesoh nah zharoo	barbecued meat
miješano meso	meejeshanoh mesoh	mixed grilled meats
na žaru	nah zharoo	barbecued
ocat	otsat	vinegar
palačinke	palacheenkay	pancakes
papar	papar	pepper
pečeno	pechenoh	baked
piletina	peeleteenah	chicken
plava riba	plavah reebah	"blue" fish
predjelo	predyeloh	starters
prilog	preelog	side dish
pršut	prshoot	smoked ham
pržene lignje	przhene leegnyey	fried squid
prženo	przhenoh	fried
ramsteak	ramsteyk	rump steak
ražnjići	razhnyeechee	pork kebabs
riba na žaru	reebah nah zharoo	barbecued fish
rižot frutti di mare	reezhot frootee dee marey	seafood risotto
rižot sa škampima	reezhot sah shkampeemah	scampi risotto
salata	salatah	salad
salata od hobotnice	salatah od hobotneetsey	octopus salad
sarma	sarmah	stuffed cabbage leaves
sir	seer	cheese
sladoled	sladoled	ice cream
slana srdela	slanah srdelah	salted sardines
škampi na buzaru	shkampee nah boozaroo	scampi in tomato and onion sauce
školjke na buzaru	shkolkay nah boozaroo	shellfish in tomato sauce
špageti frutti di mare	shpagetee frootee dee marey	spaghetti with seafood
sol	sol	salt
tjestenina	tjesteneenah	pasta
ulje	oolyey	oil

Drinks

bijelo vino	beeyeloh veenoh	white wine
crno vino	tsrnoh veenoh	red wine
gazirana/ negazirana mineralna voda	gazeeranah/ neygazeeranah meeneralnah vodah	sparkling/still mineral water
čaj	ch-igh	tea
kava	kavah	coffee
pivo	peevoh	beer

Numbers

0	nula	noolah
1	jedan	yedan
2	dva	dvah
3	tri	tree
4	četiri	cheteeree
5	pet	pet
6	šest	shest
7	sedam	sedam
8	osam	osam
9	devet	devet
10	deset	deset
11	jedanaest	yedanighst
12	dvanaest	dvahnighst
13	trinaest	treenighst
14	četrnaest	chetrnighst
15	petnaest	petnighst
16	šesnaest	shestnighst
17	sedamnaest	sedamnighst
18	osamnaest	osamnighst
19	devetnaest	devetnighst
20	dvadeset	dvahdeset
21	dvadeset i jedan	dvahdeset ee yedan
30	trideset	treedeset
31	trideset i jedan	treedeset ee yedan
40	četrdeset	chetrdeset
50	pedeset	pedeset
60	šezdeset	shezdeset
70	sedamdeset	sedamdeset
80	osamdeset	osamdeset
90	devedeset	devedeset
100	sto	stoh
101	sto i jedan	stoh ee yedan
102	sto i dva	stoh ee dvah
200	dvjesto	dvyestoh
500	petsto	petstoh
700	sedamsto	sedamstoh
900	devetsto	devetstoh
1,000	tisuću	teesoochoo

Time

One minute	jedna minuta	yednah meenootah
One hour	jedan sat	yedan saht
Half an hour	pola sata	polah sahtah
Monday	ponedjeljak	ponedyelyak
Tuesday	utorak	ootorak
Wednesday	srijeda	sreejedah
Thursday	četvrtak	chetvrtak
Friday	petak	petak
Saturday	subota	soobotah
Sunday	nedjelja	nedyelyah

Central and Southern Dalmatia Map Index

Dubrovnik Old Town Map Index